Five Steps to a PMS-Free Life

5 STEPS to a PMS-Free Life

The groundbreaking new program that stops the monthly roller coaster and puts *you* in control

George J. Kallins, M.D. & Gloria Keeling

Village Healer Press

Laguna Niguel, California

Published by
VILLAGE HEALER PRESS
Publisher: Bettina Polydor Kallins
23996 Dory Drive
Laguna Niguel, CA 92677
www.villagehealerpress.com

Distributed to the trade by National Book Network

The advice and suggestions contained in this book are not intended to replace medical care. Please consult with your physician before altering any prescribed medications or regimens.

Project Editor: Mary Monroe
Editors: Jody Berman, Joann Bally
Cover: Irene Zevgolis. *Cover photo courtesy of Corbis Images*
Illustrations: Robert Duron, Craig Swanson
Interior design & production: Polly Christensen
Index: Gwen Gotsch
Logo design: Thoma Kiki

International Standard Book Number: 0-9678988-0-3

Kallins, George J.
    Five steps to a PMS-free life : the
groundbreaking new program that stops the monthly
roller coaster and puts you in control / George J.
Kallins & Gloria Keeling
    5 steps to a PMS-free life -- 1st ed.
    p.cm. -- (the busy woman's guide)
    5 steps to a PMS-free life
    includes bibliographic references and index.
    ISBN: 0-9678988-0-3

    I. Premenstrual syndrome--Treatment.
    1. Keeling, Gloria. II. Title. III. Title: 5 steps
to a PMS-free life

    RG165.K35 2000   618.1'72
                            QB100-500114

10 9 8 7 6 5 4 3 2 1

Printed and bound in the United States by Edwards Brothers

Contents

About the Authors

GEORGE J. KALLINS, M.D., is the former director of the Center for Women's Mood Disorders at the University of Southern California Keck School of Medicine. Currently, he is Assistant Clinical Professor of Obstetrics and Gynecology at USC Keck School of Medicine. Before joining the faculty, Dr. Kallins was in private practice in Mission Viejo, California, near Los Angeles. Over the past nine years, he has researched and lectured on premenstrual syndrome as well as other women's issues. Dr. Kallins received a B.S. degree in Psychobiology from the University of Southern California in Los Angeles where he graduated Phi Beta Kappa. He went on to earn his degree in medicine from Rush University, Rush Medical College in Chicago, Illinois. Dr. Kallins and his wife Bettina live in Laguna Beach, California, where he is an avid jogger and fitness enthusiast.

GLORIA KEELING began her career in fitness in 1963 in the original open weight-training pen in Venice Beach, California. She went on to initiate weight-training programs for women at YMCAs in both Northern and Southern California. After moving to Maui, Hawaii, in 1970, Gloria began her in-depth training in yoga, aerobics, t'ai chi, dance and meditation. In 1980 she founded the Strong, Stretched & Centered Mind/Body Fitness Training Institute, the first integrated vocational training program for fitness instructors. With graduates in thirty-five countries, the Maui program is still unique in the world. As a leader in the field of mind/body healing for over three decades, Gloria lectures and gives workshops worldwide.

She is a regular contributor to *Benning's Health and Fitness Journal.* Gloria resides in Los Angeles, California where she works with private clients, writes and plays with her two grandsons.

Acknowledgments

My deepest thanks to my patients at Mission Hospital, San Clemente Hospital, Saddleback College Clinic, and at USC—you inspired this book. I hope that this five-step program can in turn inspire many other women to heal themselves and improve their lives.

Dr. Dan Michel has been an admired mentor and fount of inspiration throughout my career. Dr. William and Martha Sears have generously shared wise and witty advice on the foray into authorhood. Jed Lyons and his NBN team have been tireless champions of my book, as have my publicist Laura Deal and the entire Village Healer Press team.

This project has soared as a result of the hard work and talent of my co-author, Gloria Keeling. Gloria lives her life every day as she teaches. I hope that more of us in the medical profession can learn from her example. And also, Mary Monroe, your positive spirit and editing genius are much appreciated.

To my wife and soulmate, Bettina, without you this project would not have been possible.

—GEORGE J. KALLINS, M.D.

I am so grateful for the opportunity to introduce this life-enhancing information to women. Of the many people who helped make my participation in this book possible, the foremost are Dr. George and Bettina Kallins. I want to thank them for their bravery and ongoing support and guidance.

The five steps program would not exist for me without the editing (more like co-writing) of my dear friend, Mary Monroe. The lightheartedness with which she approaches the hard work of writing puts it all in perspective.

The tradition in mind-body arts is to honor the lineage of your teachers. In that spirit, I want to thank my many gifted yoga and t'ai chi instructors, who have each become a part of me. During my thirty-five years as a teacher, I have learned as much from my students as they have from me, and I thank them for constantly requiring that I grow beyond my self-imposed limits so they can grow beyond theirs.

Without the devoted staff of the Strong, Stretched & Centered Mind/Body Fitness Training Institute I wouldn't have the time to write. Thanks, friends, for taking the torch, especially Roan and Emily Marshall and Paula and Bill Keele. Special thanks to Claudia Micco who helped SS&C and myself grow into maturity.

My entire family inspires me but my son, Gregory, has inspired me more than anyone in my life, and taught me focus and determination. Mom—who at 82 works out every day—shows us all how great life can be at every stage. My sister Stephenie, who has published two wonderful books, showed me that, with a lot of hard work, it really can be done. Finally, hooray for my daughter-in-law, Jana, and grandsons William and Joseph, who make it all fun and love-filled.

—GLORIA KEELING

Foreword

I first met Gloria Keeling nearly ten years ago at the Las Vegas Hilton, where we were both attending a large international convention for fitness professionals. I was there as a fitness writer, and I recognized her immediately as the famed founder of the groundbreaking Strong, Stretched & Centered Mind/Body Fitness Training Institute in Maui. She was well known in the industry for being ahead of her time, a pioneer in the mind-body-spirit principles that would eventually move into the mainstream of health care. Yet, as we were introduced, she seemed more like an old friend than an industry visionary. "Being cooped up in this air conditioning and these crowds is driving me crazy," she confided (it was July). "I miss fresh air. I miss the quiet country road outside of my house." I would later visit her little house in Maui, with its overgrown tropical jungle of a backyard, skittering geckos for pets and walls covered with notes and gifts from hundreds of grateful students.

As our friendship grew, I quickly learned that Gloria is a woman who makes and follows her own path, whether it is on her beloved island, in Los Angeles where she currently lives or into bold new territory in the field of health and fitness.

Over the last decade I have also learned that Gloria is a woman who believes in other women and their power to shape their own lives. Whenever I have hesitated to take an important step in my own life, she has reminded me that, "once I make the leap, the rest will follow." So it isn't surprising that Gloria has dedicated herself to helping women make the leap to self-empowered recovery from one of the most underexplored health concerns of women's lives: PMS. On this much-needed mission, she has found the perfect partner, George Kallins, M.D., the noted California obstetrics and gynecology expert who has helped countless women overcome PMS. Dr. George (as he is fondly known to friends) and Gloria offer women, and the people who love them, validation of their experience. For too long, the painful and frustrating challenges of PMS have been doubted, trivialized, ignored and denied. Dr. George and Gloria speak compassionately and respectfully to the nearly 6 million women nationwide who struggle with PMS, and who lose more than six years of their lives to its far-ranging symptoms. In *5 Steps to a PMS-Free Life,* they offer a creative and practical strategy that every woman with PMS symptoms can tailor to her individual needs. Best of all, their groundbreaking program doesn't just offer typical answers from mainstream medicine or new solutions from the forefront of mind-body health and fitness. Instead, it combines the best of both.

5 Steps to a PMS-Free Life is an empowering, validating tool for women and a welcome step forward in women's health care. Every woman may not be fortunate enough, as I have been, to personally work with Gloria and Dr. George as they guide and inspire women to improve the health and quality of their lives. But every woman can take *5 Steps to a PMS-Free Life* and make it part of her own personal journey to greater health, happiness and fulfillment.

—MARY MONROE
Editorial Director,
Benning's Health & Fitness Journal

Introduction: You Can Take Control

GEORGE J. KALLINS, M.D.
& GLORIA KEELING

YOU HAVE IN YOUR HANDS a powerful tool: a proven five-step program to conquer premenstrual syndrome (PMS), enhance your productivity and improve the quality of your life. A cross-section of women from all walks of life and at every stage of their childbearing years experience PMS. Unfortunately, until now, there has been no solution practical enough to fit into busy women's schedules and comprehensive enough to make a real difference in the many areas of life that can be impacted by PMS.

Because modern research is rapidly unraveling the complex interactions of mind and body, we are now able to devise a multifaceted solution for one of the most real and perplexing problems in women's health. This five-step program is the first to blend medicine with the healing properties of mind-body practices and informed self-care. It recognizes both the individual nature of PMS symptoms and treatment and the demanding realities of busy women's lives.

We believe the combined force of these strategies can empower you to take charge of your health and your life in all aspects:

physical, mental, emotional and spiritual. The benefit for you—and for millions of other women who share this health challenge—is enormous: daily living with greater control, clarity and freedom from the limitations of PMS.

PMS Unveiled: Do You Have PMS?

Whether you are a twenty-one-year-old student, a thirty-something mom or a professional woman in her forties, chances are you have felt some degree of irritability, moodiness, bloating or the many other symptoms that can be attributed to PMS. If these symptoms are mildly troublesome and infrequent, you are fortunate. If these symptoms are debilitating and appear relentlessly month after month, you are not alone.

According to the American College of Obstetrics and Gynecology (ACOG), symptoms of PMS occur in up to 80 percent of all women of reproductive age. Symptoms are described as severe or debilitating in 5 to 20 percent of all women. The effect of such a ubiquitous problem is staggering: this large segment of the population loses as much as two months each year to PMS-related complications that have a significant negative impact on health and well-being, productivity, relationships and quality of life. No wonder PMS has been referred to as "the world's most common disease"!

Yet—and this may be the most astonishing fact of all—PMS remains underdiagnosed and undertreated. Few physicians are trained to diagnose PMS, and women are constantly being bombarded by conflicting and often inaccurate explanations of PMS and its treatment. A 1998 survey of over 200 women, published in the September issue of the *Journal of Women's Health,* found that most of the women surveyed did not feel their physicians were adequately informed to treat them; only one in four believed they found a treatment that was helpful; three out of four made the initial diagnosis themselves; and only 35 percent reported being "very satisfied" with their current treatment. Clearly, we have a long way to go in successfully treating PMS.

It wasn't long ago that PMS went unrecognized altogether, the implication too often being that PMS was imaginary, a feminine weakness or a condition women in some way brought on themselves. To the contrary, some premenstrual women experience increased energy, greater sexual drive and enhanced creativity. PMS stokes the fire. We intend, with the five steps program, to help you be one of these lucky ones. Your hormonal changes can work for you rather than against you.

There Is A Better Way

We wanted to develop a brand new PMS approach that would finally bridge the gap that has long existed between the millions of women who suffer from PMS and the strategies that can bring both relief and participation in the treatment process. As Gloria has often said, after watching and listening to stories of the damaging effects of PMS suffered by so many women who receive little or no satisfactory treatment, "There has to be a better way!"

So, as a team, we decided to create a new kind of integrative program that combines both of our areas of expertise: Dr. Kallins' experience as a physician in clinical practice as well as a researcher and lecturer on treatment for women's health issues, and Gloria's work as a pioneer in mind-body fitness and health,

George J. Kallins, M.D., is the former director of the Center for Women's Mood Disorders at the University of Southern California School of Medicine in Los Angeles, California. Dr. Kallins has spent the past decade helping thousands of women with PMS in his clinical practice, in addition to extensive researching and lecturing on premenstrual syndrome and related woman's health issues including menopause, perimenopause and postpartum depression.

In his clinical practice, Dr. Kallins has found that the majority of patients are lacking the most current and critical information they need to free themselves from the daunting limitations imposed by PMS. Consequently, he has worked to empower his patients with emerging developments in medicine and mind-body health.

In Gloria's years as a mind-body fitness and health instructor, lecturer and author, and as the founder of the first professional mind-body fitness instruction program, the Strong, Stretched & Centered Mind/Body Institute (SS&C) in Maui, Hawaii, she has worked with literally thousands of women between the ages of eighteen and fifty-five.

In teaching the principles of yoga, t'ai chi and other mind-body health and fitness practices in many countries around the world, she has observed a distinct connection between the healing properties of these techniques and numerous symptoms of PMS. And she's found that empowering women with the tools to take charge of their own health can create deep and lasting life changes that go far beyond freedom from PMS.

The excellent results Dr. Kallins has had in his practice, the supporting research from other scientists in this medical field, and Gloria's own pioneering research and experience in mind-body fitness and health are the foundation of this groundbreaking five-step program.

Eight Program Principles

Five Steps to a PMS-Free Life is a radically new approach: for the first time, it brings together the best of medicine and mind-body health to comprehensively address PMS with a practical plan of treatment. The basis of our program is a synergistic blend of eight key principles that re-define how we view and treat PMS:

1. PMS is real, complex, and treatable. This is the underlying principle of the five-step program: PMS is a serious problem that should not be ignored and is treatable. The era of doubting its existence, minimizing its effects or trivializing treatment is over. In fact, premenstrual dysphoric disorder (PMDD), which includes symptoms of anger/irritability, depressed mood, anxiety/tension, decreased energy and eating problems has been included in the latest edition of the *Diagnostic and Statistical Manual of Mental Disorders.* The full spectrum of potential related health and quality of life issues has yet to be determined (one research study, for example, has suggested that PMS is linked to a variety of problems in perimenopause), but there is no longer any doubt that PMS is a serious health issue and requires careful attention to treatment.

2. PMS must be viewed in terms of brain involvement rather than simply in terms of mechanics of the reproductive system. As Dr. Kallins points out, one of the most intriguing developments in PMS treatment is the awareness that many symptoms appear to originate in the brain, involving the regulation of neurotransmitters. This opens up a new area of treatment that includes the use of mind-body health strategies which address the mind-body connection, as well as the use of selective serotonin reuptake inhibitors (SSRIs) such as Prozac (fluoxetine), Paxil (paroxetine), Zoloft (sertraline) and Celexa (citalopram). This five-step program innovatively blends both of these dimensions of treatment.

3. Old treatments of PMS need to be re-considered. It is time to recognize new PMS strategies that really work. Dr. Kallins notes that in his experience and in research studies, conventional progesterone treatments, such as vaginal suppositories, the most widely used medical treatment for PMS in the past, have been shown to be no more effective than placebos. In fact, in spite of its popularity as a treatment, there is no scientific evidence that progesterone of any type is effective for relieving PMS symptoms. The American College of Obstetrics and Gynecology points out that there is no evidence that PMS is associated with either an excess or deficiency of estrogen. Old, ineffective theories of PMS treatment need to be retired and replaced with a results-oriented approach.

4. Regular exercise is an essential part of PMS treatment. In both Gloria's and Dr. Kallins' experience, exercise plays a critical role in creating a PMS-free life. Research has also validated that aerobic exercise alleviates PMS symptoms significantly.

5. Mind-body exercise, such as yoga, t'ai chi and qigong, can help create a PMS-free life. Because the mind-body connection plays such a fundamental role in PMS, mind-body exercise offers critical benefits in PMS treatment. In addition to providing needed stress management skills and other mental, emotional and spiritual benefits, mind-body exercise may even help you strengthen and maintain your commitment to other healthy lifestyle changes.

6. Stress makes PMS worse, and stress management techniques are critical in managing PMS. Stress-management techniques, such as those using mind-body exercise or meditation, are fundamental to achieving a PMS-free life. The relaxation response, in particular, induced by mind-body exercise or meditation, has been shown to alleviate more than 50 percent of PMS symptoms.

7. Healthy eating habits contribute immensely to a PMS-free life. Dr. Kallins has found that PMS symptoms can be greatly reduced with nutrition strategies. Research is also showing successful results with nutrition interventions; for example, calcium has been shown to be an effective component in PMS treatment. Other nutrition strategies, including the use of a variety of nutraceuticals, can be extremely helpful in designing your individual plan of PMS treatment.

8. Every woman responds differently to PMS interventions, and an effective treatment program needs to be individually tailored, with each woman playing an active role. This is the final founding principle of the five-step program: you need to take an active role in becoming PMS-free, and your action plan of treatment needs to be individualized for your particular symptoms and experience. No woman should ever settle for a one-size-fits-all solution to PMS.

We sincerely hope this program brings new health and harmony of mind, body and spirit into your life.

1 Five Steps to Freedom

GEORGE J. KALLINS, M.D
& GLORIA KEELING

Real Women Speak:

I have a close circle of friends and we have shared our PMS experiences over the past twenty years. Anyone who doubts the reality of PMS should just talk to us—we use PMS as a verb, as in, "I'm having a terrible week, I'm PMS-ing!" We've been great support for each other when no one else—including doctors, spouses, friends and family—would pay any attention. If you don't have PMS, it's hard to imagine what it's like to feel and behave so differently from one week to the next. As hard as it is to imagine, it's even harder to live through it month after month.

—Tina, public relations executive, Los Angeles, California

The worst thing about PMS is that I feel so out of control. I can't seem to concentrate on work projects. I overreact to situations at home and have a difficult time relaxing or staying calm in the face of stress. I get easily overwhelmed. All the motivation and focus I had just a few days ago disappears and suddenly I can't seem to handle even the simplest challenges, like getting dressed to go out or buying groceries. Normally, I know I'm an intelligent, capable person—but PMS really takes away my confidence.

—Marie, homemaker, Nashville, Tennessee

One of the most frustrating things about suffering from PMS was my husband's lack of understanding. He did not even believe there was such a thing. He thought it was all in my head or just an excuse to be in a bad mood. And the joke, "Are you on your period?" anytime I raised my voice or seemed a little irritated drove me nuts! It is nice to be able to show him research to validate that what I experience is typical. I can't just try harder to make it go away. My body's chemistry is making me feel the way I do. It is also reassuring for me, even though I know PMS is real, to know that I am not alone—that what I go through is normal and that there is help!

—**Andrea, law student, Boston, Massachusetts**

The degree to which I suffer from PMS has changed significantly over the past twenty years, becoming much more severe since I had children. When I was in my teens I would almost always feel sad and cry the day before my period started. Since having children, my PMS has gone from one day of suffering to four or five days. Help!

—**Carol, office manager, Princeton, New Jersey**

Change from the Inside Out

"There's something wrong—my hormones are out of whack or something ... " begin many patients in Dr. Kallins' office. They proceed with a list of diverse symptoms that are creating difficulties at work, at home, in their relationships and activities with friends, family and co-workers. They are frustrated—and baffled. Sometimes, they doubt their own instincts: *"Maybe I'm imagining it, but—"* or *"I know this sounds weird, but I feel like—"*

PMS takes a heavy toll on women's lives. In addition to the loss of control, decrease in productivity, difficulties in relationships, diminished health and well-being and general deterioration in quality of life, there is the pervading sense of feeling betrayed by your own body. This is the worst kind of betrayal, undermining your sense of feminine identity and personal power.

As Gloria notes, perhaps if our culture allowed women to naturally relax more at certain stages of the month, we would experience less anxiousness and stress. But the reality is that we have lives of constant busyness and a culture that doesn't recognize feminine biological cycles.

Fortunately, there is more help for PMS than ever before, and with the five-step program outlined here, you'll have everything you need to know to stop the hormonal roller coaster, restore your balance, relieve your stress and reinvigorate your life. This proactive plan is based on a holistic mind-body approach complemented by effective nutraceuticals and the best that contemporary medicine has to offer.

You'll find that the changes we encourage with this program are internal, rather than external, because real transformation in our health and our lives is accomplished from the inside out. The five steps of this program can lift you out of the realm of sufferer and into the role of self-healer—a very powerful experience that will carry over into other areas of your life. In addition, this program can be modified to meet your individual needs, as we know that PMS varies widely in how it impacts each individual woman.

The Big Picture

We have found that this five-step program can make a profound difference in the lives of most women, alleviating or eliminating PMS symptoms altogether:

Step 1. Treat Your Whole Self—Mind, Body and Spirit

Step 2. Find the Fitness/Freedom Connection

Step 3. Eat to Beat PMS

Step 4. Add the Nutraceuticals You Need

Step 5. Consider the Pharmaceutical Option

In the rest of this book, we will describe these steps in detail, providing you with practical action plans to take full advantage of the PMS relief available to you.

We also encourage you to further research these areas on your own, particularly as new research is released, because the foundation of this program is your willingness to be responsible for your own health and to seek the multifaceted plan of treatment that best meets your individual needs.

Slow and Steady Wins

Reading this book will, we hope, inspire you to examine and modify your lifestyle, and make lasting changes in your exercise, eating and stress management habits. But before you go out and spend big bucks at the health-food store, it would be wise to make a plan for putting these changes into effect. We all know how easy it is to plunge into the latest diet or exercise fad, but we also know just how long these enthusiasms usually last! Trying to change too much too quickly is a prescription for failure. All too soon the pendulum swings back in the other direction, and the brief excursion into healthier living ends.

If you're a typically busy modern woman, you may be wondering just how you're going to fit all the suggestions in this book into your cramped schedule. Maybe you're more skeptical about change, and understand yourself well enough to want to set realistic goals for yourself. Finding time for an hour of meditation or aerobics each day sounds like a great idea, but where would you find that hour?

Whether you're an enthusiast or a skeptic, we suggest that you introduce the changes in this book into your life gradually with small, do-able steps. Choose one or two that appeal most to you and start with these. For example, to begin, you might set aside twenty minutes for meditation each day, and cut back on the refined sugar in your diet. Maybe you already take a daily walk. Build on this by increasing the intensity of your walking workout, and walk farther, faster or move up to a jog.

As you begin to see results from these simple changes, you'll want to do more. You'll discover you can practice diaphragmatic breathing while sitting in your car at stoplights. You'll find a yoga or a t'ai chi class in your community. You'll start reading vegetarian cookbooks and find tasty ways to incorporate tofu into your meals. You'll learn more about all the nutraceuticals on the shelf at the health-food store.

You will soon be able to discern which of these steps are most effective in controlling your PMS symptoms and which changes work well in your daily life. Feeling calmer and more in control as the start of your period approaches each month will be a welcome reward for your efforts. Not having to endure the physical and emotional turmoil of PMS will keep you on track in this healthier way of life.

You may have an occasional bad month even after incorporating these steps into your life. This might happen when, for one reason or another, you slip up and don't get enough exercise or don't follow the mind-body routine that helps you control your stress. Pressures or problems in your life may also intensify PMS symptoms from time to time. Don't give up when this happens, and don't waste energy on blaming yourself or feeling guilty. Just get back into your good habits. How you feel really is under your control!

Free and Clear of PMS Forever

Life is full of challenges. How you handle them determines your character and your life path. PMS is one of the biggest challenges many women face. We suggest that you try the natural, healthy approach we outline here for three months, using the journals we describe at the end of Chapter 2 and at the end of Chapter 8. You'll be surprised at what happens when you take even a little time every day for self-healing. Your results will be based in large part on the willingness, open-mindedness and courage you bring to this program. PMS is a real and complex disease, but it is far from hopeless or untreatable. We have seen many women turn their lives around with this plan, and we believe you can, too.

I did the mind-body fitness training developed by Gloria Keeling in 1985 and up until that time I had suffered from bad PMS. My doctor had put me on the birth control pill to help control it but I hated the side effects. During the training I gave up the pill, coffee and processed food and really got into the yoga, breathing and visualization. While we held the postures, the instructor would talk about their benefits. I would visualize my reproductive organs healthy and functioning without pain. I think everything helped—but especially the visualization. The idea that the mind could help heal the body was a revelation to me in 1985. I've never looked back, but to this day if I skip my yoga for more than a week and drink coffee regularly, the PMS returns.

—Claudia, Maui, Hawaii

After following Dr. Kallins' program, I finally discovered what it's like to not have my life controlled by PMS! It feels like a miracle! I take calcium, do t'ai chi, run three times a week and make sure I eat plenty of soy protein and other healthy foods. I made the changes a little at a time, and now they're second nature to me. It's easy to do when the benefits are so great!

—Renee, Dana Point, California

I did all five steps of Dr. Kallins' program and my life has changed completely. My family can't believe the difference. Exercise and better eating habits took care of a lot of my symptoms, and taking antidepressants for part of the month also seems to work for me. I had just about given up on ever finding a solution to my PMS, but now I'm so glad I didn't!

—Dawn, Pasadena, California

The yoga I learned at Gloria Keeling's program is so beneficial for tension release prior to menstruation, gently massaging the internal organs and stretching to ease the buildup of tension in the lower back and neck area. Also the visualization of well-being as the outcome of the yoga and meditation helped calm my mind and body. The healthy diet with low-fat dairy products helped the bloating and pelvic pressure and seemed to contribute to an easier flow. I also believe that evening primrose oil/starflower oil with vitamin E contributed to a reduction in breast swelling. I ran out of these a couple of months ago and the swelling returned.

—Susan, Antigua, Caribbean

2 Straight Talk: Why You Feel the Way You Do

GEORGE J. KALLINS, M.D.

IT HAPPENS EVERY MONTH. About eight to ten days before your period starts, you notice the symptoms. Maybe you cry for no apparent reason. Maybe you're anxious or short tempered or depressed. Many women complain of bloating and breast tenderness. Others crave sweets, especially chocolate, and salty snacks. Then your period appears and miraculously, your symptoms disappear—until next month, when you can look forward to a repeat performance.

What Is PMS?

Premenstrual Syndrome (PMS) is a term used to describe physical or behavioral changes that many women experience in the days before their menstrual bleeding begins. It may appear anywhere from one to fourteen days before the beginning of menstruation. Approximately 80 percent of all women have some symptoms each month. Approximately 50 percent of all women have significant symptoms that bother them enough to describe them as a syndrome or problem. Approximately 5 percent of all women have premenstrual symptoms so severe that they are incapacitated.

Hundreds of symptoms have been reported to be associated with premenstrual syndrome. Although no one individual has all of the symptoms that have been described, most women complain of more than one problem. Because of its complexity, premenstrual syndrome has baffled individual women and their physicians for a long time. But now, as physicians and sufferers alike have developed a better understanding of PMS and the mind-body connection behind it, they have also discovered effective ways to deal with the symptoms.

The Normal Menstrual Cycle

In order to understand PMS better you first need to understand the menstrual cycle. With an understanding of the different parts of the menstrual cycle, it is easier to identify problems that are associated with particular parts of that cycle. Knowledge is power and if you have a working knowledge of the cycles of PMS, you will be more effective in using the information in this book.

Most women will never forget when they first got their period. This is a very important time because the way the members of your family handle the first menses can influence how you feel about your body for the rest of your life. There are many euphemisms for menstruation and they reflect the healthy or unhealthy attitudes people assume. For instance "the rag" or "the curse" are not uncommon among people who denigrate and/or fear this monthly process. Other, friendlier attitudes may result in "the monthly visitor" or "her friend." Stop for a moment and think about what kind of messages you got from the important people in your life. Was there shame? Did it go relatively unnoticed? Were you encouraged to think of it as remarkable, something to be celebrated?

Menstruation usually begins around the age of twelve and

continues until around the age of fifty, when most women enter menopause. For approximately thirty-eight years, women menstruate, with all of the realities associated with that—PMS being one of the most common. In some cultures the onset of menses is a time for the entire group to celebrate; it's the most important rite of passage a woman experiences. It means she can take her place as an adult; she can reproduce. Everyone participates, and there is great honor and respect given to her. All of the psychological messages she receives are positive.

Contrast this with our culture. No fabulous celebrations. No days of feasting and honoring the girl who has become a woman. Instead, we get messages of shame from ads that hype "pads so slim they are undetectable" and messages of pain from ads that extol drugs for relief. This may well set us up for unhealthy mental attitudes toward our bodies. That, combined with the high stress, poor nutrition and sedentary lifestyles of today, contributes to PMS.

The normal menstrual cycle actually is a complex and fascinating physiologic event. It involves complex communication between the brain, the pituitary gland, the ovaries and the uterus, all of which work together to prepare the body to grow a baby. Let's take a closer look at the menstrual cycle's three phases: (1) the follicular, or preovulatory phase; (2) the ovulatory phase; and (3) the luteal, or postovulatory phase.

The Preovulatory Phase

Most discussions of the menstrual cycle define day one as the first day of menstruation, or bleeding. For a woman's ovaries, these first days of the cycle are a quiet time. The ovaries released their eggs in the middle of the last cycle and at this stage are not producing large amounts of any hormones. The brain, however, is busy. The hypothalamus, a part of the brain, is beginning to release a hormone called gonadotropin-releasing hormone (GnRH), which in turn signals the pituitary gland to make follicle-stimulating hormone (FSH). FSH is released into the bloodstream and travels to the ovaries, prompting them to begin a new cycle of developing follicles, or eggs.

The Ovulatory Phase

The rising FSH levels cause eggs, or ovums, to mature. Each egg is encased in a sac called the Graafian follicle. The follicles produce estrogen, which makes the lining of the uterus grow and thicken. The final signal for ovulation comes from the brain in the form of luteinizing hormone (LH). As LH levels rise, sometime around day fourteen of a typical twenty-eight-day cycle, the sac ruptures, releasing the egg into the tube that leads to the uterus. This is called ovulation. Some women can tell when they are ovulating, because they may have some pain, typically a dull ache in the lower abdomen.

Every month approximately twenty follicles and their eggs respond to FSH and begin to ripen. Only one or perhaps two eggs actually reach the point of ovulation.

The Postovulatory Phase

After ovulation, the ruptured follicle lives on for several days. It develops into a yellow-colored gland called the corpus luteum, which produces a hormone called progesterone. Progesterone causes the uterine lining to grow; it also stimulates the breasts, causing breast tenderness and swelling. If the egg that was released is fertilized and implants itself in the uterus, the corpus luteum lives on for weeks. It is actually essential for the survival of the fetus. In the absence of pregnancy, the corpus luteum deteriorates for approximately the next ten days. Hormone levels fall, menstruation (the sloughing off of the uterine lining) begins and the cycle repeats itself.

It is in the postovulatory phase that women experience premenstrual syndrome. This is a very important concept to understand when learning about or discussing PMS. Symptoms can be attributed to PMS only when they occur every month in the fourteen days preceding the first day of the menstrual cycle, in other words, in the fourteen days before bleeding, or when menstruation begins.

The menstrual cycle depends on communication between the brain, the pituitary gland and the ovaries. This kind of complex contact between the brain and body is quite sensitive to the environment. The ovary is constantly monitoring its environment. It will listen to the body to determine whether it should release an egg—sort of nature's way of determining whether it is a good time to conceive! For example, you may fail to ovulate or take longer to ovulate when you are sick with the flu. This will cause you to either miss a period or have your period later than usual. The same principle explains why athletes or dancers may not have periods at all until they cut back on their workouts or increase their body fat. Their brains and ovaries have assessed the situation and determined that their bodies are too stressed to sustain a pregnancy.

Understanding this mind-body relationship is very important to understanding both premenstrual syndrome and its treatment. In this book, you'll find that the suggestions for treating and preventing premenstrual symptoms address this relationship directly, as well as the mind and body individually. By influencing the mind, you can change how the body feels. By nourishing the body better, you can improve the way the mind works. When you work on the mind-body relationship behind PMS, you can gain control over your symptoms and not be bothered by them any longer.

Symptoms

In the past, physicians often told women that the problems women experienced in the days before their periods were "all in their head." This didn't make the problems go away. It is only in the recent past that physicians have taken women's complaints about premenstrual syndrome seriously.

Premenstrual symptoms were first described as a medical condition in 1931 when Robert T. Frank, M.D., wrote about the subject in a medical journal and coined the term *premenstrual tension*. Dr. Frank believed that the behavioral problems were caused by an excess of ovarian hormones and recommended the use of Epsom salts to eliminate this excess. The term *premenstrual syndrome* was first used in 1953 by Katharina Dalton, M.D.

Over the past twenty years, premenstrual syndrome has received a lot of attention in the popular media. This has generated a surge in the demand for treatment. Public awareness has also caused PMS to become the subject of many jokes. Although humor can help lighten a stressful moment, PMS itself is no joke. This is demonstrated most dramatically by the fact that premenstrual syndrome has been used as a defense in murder trials and can be blamed for many crippled relationships and broken marriages.

When evaluating possible PMS symptoms, it is more important to study the timing of the symptoms rather than the symptoms themselves. We cannot overemphasize the importance of this. Symptoms that recur month after month in the fourteen days preceding a woman's menstrual cycle and that disappear at the onset of menses must be taken seriously as premenstrual syndrome. The nature of the symptoms themselves is actually less important, especially because over 150 PMS symptoms have been described. The chart that follows lists some of the most common symptoms:

PMS Symptoms

Physical	Mental	Emotional	Behavioral
Bloating	Suicidal thoughts	Anxiety	Food cravings
Breast tenderness	Sensitivity to rejection	Irritability	Social isolation
Breast swelling	Decreased concentration	Sadness	Verbally abusive to others
Weight gain		Mood swings	Physically abusive to others
Headache	Forgetfulness	Anger	
Fatigue	Feeling overwhelmed	Depression	Lack of motivation
Joint pain			Overly critical of others
Constipation	Feeling out of control		Self-mutilation

Premenstrual Dysphoric Disorder

As we mentioned earlier, approximately 5 percent of all women suffer from severe PMS. Their symptoms interfere with their day-to-day functioning. The American Psychiatric Association differentiated this type of premenstrual syndrome from less drastic cases by giving this type its own name: premenstrual dysphoric disorder (PMDD). With PMDD, you may not be able to work, sleep or interact well with other individuals during the days preceding menstruation. Women with PMDD are literally disabled for a few days every month. Like clockwork, however, their symptoms disappear when their periods start.

The PMS Puzzle

The causes of PMS are still unclear. It is very difficult for women to find consistent explanations and treatment suggestions for PMS. You may read different books and see various experts and receive entirely different answers from each source.

Many of my colleagues believe that premenstrual syndrome is

related to a deficiency in progesterone levels. This information has never been substantiated. More important, in double-blind studies, progesterone treatment for premenstrual syndrome has fared no better than placebos. My clinical observations reinforce these findings. For most of my patients, I have found that progesterone does not work. But I have had tremendous success treating my patients with calcium.

> *When Dr. Kallins first took me off progesterone, I was skeptical. I had come to him upon the recommendation of my sister-in-law who had seen great improvement with Dr. Kallins' 5-Step program. My previous Ob/Gyn had me on progesterone for years. When I tried the calcium, I noticed results in a matter of only a few weeks. It was as if a cloud had lifted! Calcium turned out to be the magic bullet for me!"*
>
> **—Lisa, mother of two, Oceanside, California**

Recent studies have demonstrated that disturbances in calcium regulation may be the root of premenstrual syndrome and that calcium supplementation may be an effective treatment. A study conducted by Susan Thys-Jacobs, M.D., and published in the August 1998 issue of *American Journal of Obstetrics and Gynecology* showed that women who took 1,200 milligrams (mg) of calcium per day had a 50 percent decrease in their experience of four major PMS symptoms: mood swings, pain, water retention and food cravings.

Although it is too soon to say for sure, there are good reasons to believe that abnormalities in how the body handles calcium and vitamin D may be responsible for the symptoms of PMS. When calcium levels are deficient, parathyroid hormone levels may be elevated, and these changes have been associated with disturbances such as depression and psychosis. Parathyroid hormone has also been linked to the regulation of serotonin in the brain. Problems with serotonin levels are also associated with depression.

Another possible influence on premenstrual syndrome may be stress. Although stress probably is not the underlying cause of premenstrual syndrome, at the very least, it plays a role in aggravating it or worsening the symptoms. Stress as a cause of disease has been underemphasized in modern medicine, yet most of us know how powerful an impact stress can have on our daily lives, our mood and our health. Many studies have shown that stress-management techniques have been very beneficial in the management of premenstrual syndrome. One study published in the April 1990 issue of *Journal of Obstetrics and Gynecology* showed that the use of stress management techniques resulted in a 58 percent reduction in symptoms of premenstrual syndrome.

Although the cause of premenstrual syndrome remains a mystery, it is possible to take what we *do* know and create a personal program of treatment. This book will give you five practical steps to help you rid yourself of the most common disease experienced by women.

As part of your efforts to take control of your health and manage your PMS symptoms, we suggest you work with your physician as well as other health-care professionals (nutritionists, psychologists, fitness professionals, etc.) to develop the program that works best for you.

Before embarking on our five-step plan, you must be certain that it is indeed PMS that you are experiencing. Often, conditions such as thyroid disorder can appear as PMS. Only a qualified physician can perform the evaluation and tests to rule out these other conditions.

Your Journal of Self-Discovery

To determine if symptoms that trouble you are caused by PMS, it is necessary to chart the symptoms throughout your cycle. If you have not already done so, you will want to begin your symptoms chart immediately, using the format we suggest here.

Along with your symptoms chart, we also suggest you begin a "journal of self-discovery" to track your observations in experiencing and treating PMS. Remember, this is an aspect of your life that will be around for some time! Writing down insights and strategies helps you remember and refine them and can also help you communicate more effectively with health-care professionals.

Symptoms Chart

For your symptoms to be considered PMS:

- You must experience the same symptoms to some degree on a monthly basis.
- Your symptoms must disappear completely or diminish several days after menstruation begins.
- Your symptoms must interfere with some aspect of daily life. This includes enjoyment.

To log your symptoms on a daily basis, buy a calendar or day planner that shows a month at a time. Get one that has large, empty spaces for each day. Each evening, reflect on your day. Using the chart on page 21, write down each of the symptoms you experienced that day. You may want to use a simple code, for instance, **E** for emotional, **P** for physical, and so on.

At the same time, begin your self-discovery journal to describe your reactions to stressful situations and your feelings from day to day. You can write about dreams and nightmares related to PMS, how you imagine life will be when you have alleviated your PMS symptoms, your questions for health-care professionals, and your ideas for creating a PMS-free future.

Of course, it is most difficult to do these tracking behaviors when you are experiencing extreme PMS! This is the time you must marshal your willpower as much as possible. It is important. Do this for three consecutive months and you will see a pattern. When you can identify exactly how PMS affects you, you will be better able to anticipate and deal with your symptoms. You will be able to modify the PMS regimen in this book to suit your particular symptoms.

3 Step 1: Treat Your Whole Self— Mind, Body & Spirit

GLORIA KEELING

WHAT MOST WOMEN DON'T KNOW about PMS is that it is a *treatable* condition. Successful treatment for most women means making some consistent lifestyle changes that don't require a great deal of extra time or money.

We have found that the most effective route to managing PMS is a holistic, multidimensional approach based on the philosophy that the body, mind and spirit are interconnected. The idea of a close connection between body and mind is a relatively new idea to American physicians, but increasingly physicians who have practiced traditional Western medicine are beginning to recommend alternative therapies to their patients for many different conditions.

In a 1998 survey conducted at Kaiser Permanente Medical Care Program in Northern California, 90 percent of the adult primary care physicians and obstetrics-gynecology clinicians reported recommending at least one alternative therapy, primarily for pain management. Chiropractic, acupuncture, massage and behavioral medicine techniques such as meditation and relaxation training were most often cited.

Even the role of spirituality and religion in promoting healing is rapidly becoming commonplace. The John Templeton Foundation, an organization that promotes research and coursework on the connection between spirituality and medicine, recently sponsored a survey of the American public, HMO professionals and family physicians. The results showed that a resounding 86 percent of Americans believe that personal prayer, meditation or other spiritual and religious practices can accelerate or help the medical treatment of people who are ill. Ninety-nine percent of family physicians and 94 percent of HMO executives agree.

Welcome Wellness

Why are health care professionals, as well as the public, increasingly embracing mind-body approaches? The three primary reasons are:

1. Documented evidence. These are far from being modern or "newfangled" ideas. Many of these techniques have been around for centuries, and mounting evidence of their effectiveness in promoting wellness can no longer be ignored. Although there is still a popular perception that benefits of mind-body therapies are not documented, this is not the case at all.

"More than 30 years of research, as well as the experiences of a large and growing number of individuals and health-care providers, suggest that meditation and similar forms of relaxation can lead to better health, higher quality of life, and lowered health care costs," says Pamela Peeke, M.D., M.P.H. While the research for complementary therapies still lags somewhat behind research of more conventional treatments, many scientists believe this is due in part to a difficulty in obtaining significant grant funding, as well as to the challenges inherent in researching complex mind-body interactions.

2. Safety. Part of the Hippocratic oath that all physicians take is the philosophy of "doing no harm." The very core of a physician's profession is to assist in the healing of the body, being careful to do no harm in the process. The beauty of alternative therapies is that they fit this philosophy exactly. Although they are powerful tools when used correctly, they generally have few or no negative side effects. This is an important consideration, particularly in light of the potential for harmful side effects that accompanies many pharmacological and surgical treatments.

This is not to say that mind-body approaches and conventional medical treatment can't work very well together. In fact, some emerging research indicates that mind-body exercises may reduce the need for medications or assist medications in doing their job.

3. Treating the person, not just the symptoms. Although Western medicine has traditionally taken a narrow approach to healing, concentrating on treating the physiological symptoms, alternative medicine addresses the whole person, body, mind and spirit to uncover the causes of symptoms. The remedies generally involve more than merely treating symptoms and can be customized for individual needs. A combination of diet, exercise, vitamins, herbs and other techniques strengthens the body, mind and spirit and helps them work better *together.*

The Mind-Body Link to PMS

Why emphasize mind-body health and exercise treatments for PMS? As science reveals that the source of many PMS symptoms appears to be associated with the mind-body interactions in the brain, the fact that mind-body treatments may positively impact these interactions holds great promise. Information processing in the brain is currently one of the most potent areas of research in medicine.

"Neuroscience has taught us much about the nature of mind-body," says Ralph La Forge, M.S., managing director of the Duke University Lipid Clinic and Disease Management Preceptorship Program at Duke University Medical Center in North Carolina and former chair of the international IDEA Mind-Body Fitness Committee. "The neuron is the most fundamental unit of information processing within the brain and there are some 80 billion-plus neurons within the adult human brain. Each receives input from 5,000 to 40,000 other neuronal axons, making the number of possible avenues of information exchanging in the brain nearly incomprehensible," says La Forge.

We still have much to learn about the impressive pathways that underlie mind-body communication. Although we are only now beginning to scientifically document this process, the connection between mind and body has been a fundamental aspect of human culture around the world. As La Forge suggests in his work ("Introduction to the Art and Science of Mind-Body Fitness," 1997), the concept of a vital life force, referred to as *chi* in China, *ki* in Japan, *prana* in India, *aether* in classical physics and *essence* or *soul* in the United States, may reflect our attempts to understand the interrelationships between mind, body and nature (or spirit.)

The impact of these neural transactions on our daily lives is indeed extraordinary, including a probable association with PMS symptoms. "For example, our perception of self or an environmental event appears to be directly related to the number of neurons, neurotransmitters and associated receptor proteins that are activated," says La Forge. "This electrochemical information is turned into the hormones of behavior by the limbic system, which includes the thalamus, hypothalamus and hippocampus. Much of this process is accomplished by the hypothalamic-pituitary-adrenal axis," he adds.

This is the route or process by which many messages move "between" mind and body—including the signals now believed to result in many PMS symptoms.

"Some research indicates that mind-body therapies such as hypnosis, t'ai chi and meditation can alter the process for the better to provide such benefits as reduced stress and improved mental clarity," notes La Forge.

This is why mind-body therapies hold promise for safe, effective and holistic treatment of PMS. In this chapter, we will describe a variety of specific ways you can use mind-body movement and meditation to decrease PMS symptoms by calming your body and mind.

Move the Mind

La Forge and the IDEA Mind-Body Exercise Committee have defined mind-body fitness as integrating these five components:

1. **Mentative,** or having a noncompetitive and nonjudgmental introspective component, which is process centered rather than strictly goal oriented.
2. **Proprioceptive awareness,** or incorporating a low-level muscular movement with mental focus on muscle and movement sense.
3. **Breath centered,** or using the breath as the primary centering activity.
4. **Anatomic alignment,** or focusing on proper physical form throughout the movements.
5. **Energy centric,** or awareness of the movement of one's intrinsic energy, life force, chi, or other described energy form.

In short, this means that mind-body activity is based on directives from inside of you rather than directions from an outside source. What you are sensing internally determines how you do the exercise. The mind-body processes we will develop in this step are designed to help you tap into your internal body knowledge.

Mind-body techniques that have originated in other cultures can help you begin to live a PMS-free life. Finding a mind-body discipline that will work for you is the first step in this PMS program.

The Relaxation Response

Herbert Benson, M.D., associate professor of medicine at the Mind/Body Medical Institute at Harvard Medical School, coined the term "relaxation response" to describe the body's own ability to calm itself. Benson explains in *The Wellness Book* that, like the fight-or-flight response to danger, the relaxation response is inborn. He describes the two as "counterbalancing mechanisms" because one generates stress in order to protect the body and the other reduces it, also to benefit the body. The fight-or-flight response is automatic. When the brain perceives a threat, it sends out stress hormones that enable a person to respond directly to the danger or to get away.

For instance, if you are walking down the street and a big dog jumps a fence and races toward you snarling, the body floods with hormones that speed the heart rate and increase muscle strength and blood pressure so that you can either climb a tree, run like hell, or fight the dog (my least likely choice).

The relaxation response does not kick in automatically, which is a problem in our high-stress culture. We are constantly producing the hormones that cause stress but not the behavior that is necessary to relieve that stress. This is very hard on the body. Fortunately for us, the relaxation response can be elicited through various techniques including diaphragmatic breathing, meditation, yoga, imagery, and slow moving exercise such as t'ai chi ch'uan. Aerobic exercise is also very good at using up the stress hormones produced so that they don't accumulate in the body and cause long-term damage. We will talk about that later in the book.

The impact of the relaxation response on premenstrual syndrome has been demonstrated in a study of forty-six women suffering from PMS. The landmark study, published in *Obstetrics and Gynecology*, stated that, "the regular elicitation of the relaxation response is an effective treatment for physical and emotional premenstrual symptoms, and is most effective in women with severe symptoms."

As you practice one or more of the techniques described in this chapter, you will discover the relaxation response for yourself. You'll find that releasing tension from your body will calm your mind and that letting go of mental activity will de-stress your body. As your mind and body become better able to work together, it is likely that your PMS symptoms will decrease. You'll notice other benefits as well. You may feel more "centered" and less overwhelmed by both the ordinary and the extraordinary events of life. Many practitioners report a sense of "connection and belonging" that eases the pain of living in our modern, often impersonal world. Coping skills increase in all areas of our lives.

Breathe Right

According to Herbert Benson, eliminating stress begins with learning how to breathe. A ludicrous idea, you may think. You've been breathing all your life! Yet paying more attention to breathing correctly is actually something from which everyone could benefit, not just PMS sufferers. Learning to manage stress and control anxiety is critically important to overall health. And proper breathing is a basic tool for achieving this goal.

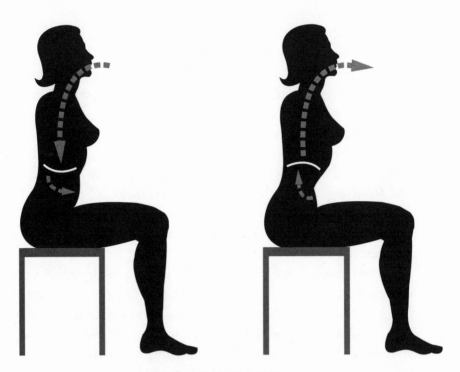

Diaphragmatic Breathing

Tension and anxiety are frequently accompanied by shallow, or "chest," breathing. This cuts us off from the vitality that is available through deep breathing. Many Eastern disciplines such as yoga from India and Zen meditation from Japan place great emphasis on diaphragm breathing as a way to bring balance to the mind and body. In yoga, deep breathing is called *pranayama*. *Prana* means breath, respiration, life, vitality, wind, energy or strength. It also connotes the soul as opposed to the body. *Ayama* means length, expansion, stretching or restraint. Pranayama thus connotes extension of breath and its control. Swami Vishnu De-vananda, respected yoga master, says, "Pranayama is the link between the mental and physical disciplines. While the action is physical, the effect is to make the mind calm, lucid and steady." Mind-body disciplines recognize that the breath is the bridge between the mind and the body. What a simple, elegant way to connect with our "self."

Breath is, after all, life. We can live for weeks without food and days without water but only minutes without breath. Unfortunately, as we age, our lungs lose their elasticity. This happens even if we are regular about our exercise. We can keep our vital capacity high, however, if we keep our breathing muscles strong with diaphragmatic breathing.

Benefits of Diaphragmatic Breathing

- **Helps cleanse the blood.** Inhaling deeply brings more oxygen into the bloodstream to be carried to the cells and used for cellular processes. The blood leaving the cells carries the waste products created by this cellular metabolism. They are partly eliminated during the exhale. In other words, the blood goes out from the lungs like a fresh stream from the mountains and returns like a sewer stream full of impurities that must be exhaled.

- **Improves circulation.** The more efficiently the blood circulates, the faster the blood cleansing process happens. This helps prevent disease. Parts of the body that don't have good circulation slowly suffocate and die.

- **Decreases the heart rate.** A fast heart rate is often the sign of a compromised cardiovascular system. Beta blocking drugs are given to slow the heart rate. We can do it naturally with mind-body techniques.

- **Lowers the metabolic rate.** This has a wonderfully calming effect on the body, and is an important aspect of the relaxation response.

- **Increases lymphatic flow.** The lymph system both eliminates impurities from the body that are too big for the bloodstream and is one of our immune system's main lines of defense. Good lymph circulation helps prevent the buildup of toxins that can result in disease.

- **Lowers blood sugar levels.** This helps get us off the roller coaster of the highs and lows of fluctuating blood sugar that can result in hypoglycemia and adult onset diabetes.
- **Reduces anxiety and hypertension.** Being anxious and having high blood pressure can result in heart disease and a shorter, less productive and less enjoyable life.
- **Helps prevent cardiovascular problems which can result in a restricted life or even a heart attack.**
- **Produces a feeling of alertness.** This natural wakefulness is much healthier for the body than the "buzz" derived from caffeine.

When our muscles get tense and contracted and our breathing becomes shallow, we are sending stress signals to the brain. As we relax and stretch the tension out of our muscles and slow down and deepen our breathing, we are calming and quieting the mind, lowering blood pressure, relaxing the heart, lowering cholesterol levels, and bringing our entire being into a balanced state.

Diaphragmatic Breathing Technique
Diaphragmatic breathing can be done anywhere, anytime. Utilize the technique as often as possible, especially when feeling stress, anger, fear or any emotional or physical pain. This exercise will elicit the relaxation response in your body and counteract the effects of what you are feeling to help you handle stressful situations better.

1. Find a warm, quiet, safe space. You want to have some time, perhaps ten to fifteen minutes, without interruptions, especially when you are first practicing diaphragmatic breathing. Sit comfortably in a straight-back chair with your feet flat on the floor and your hands on your thighs, palms up. Sit up as straight as you can without creating tension in your body. If you are very limber, you may want to sit cross-legged on a cushion on the floor, palms up, on your knees. Just be sure your back is straight so that your lungs can ex-

pand completely and there is no pressure on your organs. Using the wall for support can help. Many students find it easier to feel the breath filling and emptying when lying on their back with one hand placed on their lower abdominal muscles and the other one on their chest. Try each of these positions and find what works for you.

2. Exhale completely and begin to inhale slowly through your nose, gradually filling the lungs from the bottom to the top. As the lower lungs fill, you will feel the lower abdomen rise. As the middle lungs fill, they will expand the rib cage. As the upper lungs fill, they will lift the chest and finally the collarbones. Keep your shoulders down and relaxed.

3. Exhale slowly through your nose, first feeling the collarbones and chest fall, next the rib cage contracting, and last of all the lower abdomen drawing inward. At this point, deepen the exhale by contracting in and upward with the abdominal muscles. Now your lungs are empty and ready for another deep inhale.

4. Visualize the lungs like a vase of water filling from the bottom to the top and emptying from the top to the bottom. When first beginning diaphragm breathing, use a count of four to six for the inhale and six to eight for the exhale. Count "one, one thousand, two, one thousand, three, one thousand," and so on, to keep the count slow and consistent. If this count is too long for you to do comfortably, then adapt it to your needs. You will, through practice, build your lung capacity and be able to lengthen your count. The extended exhale is very important to empty the lungs so that you have room for the deep inhale. Therefore, if you are inhaling to the count of three, try to exhale to at least the count of four, making your exhale longer than your inhale.

In the beginning, practice only as long as you are comfortable. Doing even five to ten breaths is an excellent start; remember you're taking small, do-able steps. Eventually you can increase the time for up to twenty minutes. At this point you are practicing meditation. If you can breathe diaphragmatically for twenty minutes without losing focus, you are in deep meditation. Be loving and patient with yourself as you learn this technique.

Alternate Nostril Breathing

Every yoga teacher I have ever studied with emphasized the importance of alternate nostril breathing for the relief of PMS. This is simply diaphragmatic breathing using one nostril at a time. To do it, follow all of the steps above for diaphragmatic breathing but add this twist:

Alternate Nostril Breathing

1. After inhaling through both nostrils, use the thumb of your right hand to close the right nostril; exhale and inhale once through the left nostril using the counting method we've already learned.

2. Now close the left nostril using the ring finger of your right hand and exhale and inhale once through the right nostril keeping the same steady, relaxed count.

3. Doing one exhale and inhale through both nostrils is considered one cycle. Do between five and ten cycles in the beginning and increase for up to five minutes. Practice basic diaphragm breathing for five to ten minutes and then do five to ten cycles of alternate nostril breathing. Then sit quietly for a few moments and notice the effect on your mind and body.

Meditation to Stir Your Soul

I first encountered meditation in 1970 when I moved from Los Angeles to Maui. I was twenty-seven, and my life had been what I thought was fairly typical for a single mom living in the city. I'd been working three part-time jobs and going to school, gym training at a YMCA in the mornings, waitressing a lunch shift, going to city college in the afternoons, modeling for artists in the evenings ... oh, and doing my best to raise my nine-year-old-son. All of this without a car. I took buses everywhere, and while riding them I did my studying.

I didn't even know I was crazed until I'd gone through the "letting go" phase everyone who moves to the Islands experiences. Once I had finally unwound (by planting a garden, starting to study t'ai chi and yoga and living in a small house in the jungle without electricity or a phone), I was ready to try meditation.

Learn How to Relax

If the purpose of meditation is to enable us to experience life from a place of inner calm and peacefulness, then we have to approach it in a realistic manner. Now, I am not suggesting anyone needs to move to the Islands or live without a phone. Good grief, no! But I am suggesting it's necessary and healthy to take time off from the madness on a regular basis to learn how to be quiet and with yourself. In this section we are going to explore several different ways to do that starting with very simple awareness walking exercises and evolving into deep meditation.

People who meditate regularly have skills for coping that aren't readily available to the rest of us. When I began reviewing the literature on meditation, I constantly came across the phrase "experienced meditators." All of the studies that supply the "proof" that meditation helps many different problems, including PMS, have been done on experienced meditators. That makes perfect sense. You wouldn't study the effects of jogging on someone who's only been doing it for a couple of weeks.

There is a misconception that anyone who wants to meditate can do it quite easily. It's actually one of the most demanding practices I've encountered. In a culture that values "doing" and "results," the idea of sitting and being still or simply being "mindful," that is, paying attention to whatever is going on each moment, may seem like a waste of time. Actually it's one of the most productive ways to involve yourself in life. And if you are perceptive, you will begin to notice subtle changes almost immediately.

Meditation's Health Benefits

Numerous research studies and reviews have verified the effectiveness of meditation on a wide spectrum of stress-related health problems. When the stress hormone norepinephrine is released in the body, it triggers the fight-or-flight response. This is great if a surge of physical activity is required. But most of the stress of modern life is mental, and when the fight-or-flight response is triggered, the result is tension that is not burned away with physical release. Meditation creates the opposite effect: it activates the relaxation response, producing a state of tranquility. Studies have shown that meditation can actually lower the body's responsiveness to norepinephrine and can, therefore, help people cope with stress.

Meditation has been shown to be effective against many of the symptoms of premenstrual syndrome, such as anxiety, panic, depression and headaches. Here are some other potential benefits of this ancient practice:

- A sense of peace and serenity.
- Mental clarity.
- A calmer approach to problem solving.
- Enhanced memory.
- Diminished anger.
- Improved decision-making skills.
- Self-discipline.
- Improved overall health and well-being.
- Spiritual connectedness.

A study conducted at the University of California-Irvine in 1977 tested the effects of mindfulness meditation on stress reduction. The researchers concluded that "techniques of mindfulness meditation, with their emphasis on developing detached observation and awareness of the contents of consciousness, may represent a powerful cognitive behavioral coping strategy for transforming the ways in which we respond to life events."

At the University of Massachusetts, a recent study on anxiety revealed that twenty out of twenty-two anxiety-prone volunteers showed marked improvement after taking an eight-week class in meditation.

A 1997 study of the particular technique known as Transcendental Meditation (TM) examined its impact on the levels of stress hormones. The results showed that the body responds to meditation with a reduction of stress hormones, leading the researchers to suggest that the "repeated practice of the TM technique reverses effects of chronic stress significant for health." The effects of meditation can also be demonstrated by looking at the flow of electrical impulses through in the brain. Studies with an electroencephalograph (EEG) have shown that meditation boosts the intensity of alpha waves associated with quiet, receptive states. This produces a state of calm not even seen during sleep. Many long-time meditators, myself included, experience meditation as more restful than sleep.

Making Meditation a Part of Your Life

It's important to understand that there are many different ways of practicing meditation. I will give you a variety of choices so you can discover what calms you down and gives you a sense of inner peace. Each of us has a different lifestyle and is at a different place in our development. If we are to integrate meditation as a lifetime practice, we need to find our own path. As we become comfortable with one form, we can move on and master another, eventually working our way to completely still, seated meditation.

As you experiment with the various kinds of meditations in this section, remember to use small, do-able steps. Take time with each form. Changing how your mind perceives reality is a process that deserves patience. Be as gentle with yourself as you would with a small child learning a new skill. The beginning stage of mastering anything new is a very challenging and exciting time. Be sure you take a few minutes every day to write in your journal of self-discovery. These processes are like holding a mirror on ourself that reflects what is going on inside. You will learn a lot and want to remember. In a couple of years this new way of being will seem so natural, you'll feel as if you've been here all your life.

A Myriad of Forms

My Webster's dictionary defines meditation as "contemplation or reflection ... to focus one's thoughts on: reflect on or ponder over ... to plan or project in the mind." If we believe this definition, it sounds like the mind is busy during meditation. This is true of certain forms of meditation, but the long-term goal is to detach from our thoughts and unplug completely from our small self, or ego, and plug into our higher self, which is directly connected to God, or universal energy, or the cosmos; or whatever you label The Big Picture.

It is only when we detach from our thoughts that we achieve the brain state that is more restful than sleep. However, every kind and stage of meditation helps relieve symptoms of PMS such as stress and anxiety. So begin with any one of these. Just begin.

Living Daily Life in a "Flow State"

One of the most basic kinds of meditation is experienced without even trying. It is something most of us are familiar with if we stop and think about it. People involved in creativity are "in the flow" often, usually when their work is unfolding easily. It simply means that we are so completely absorbed in what we are doing that we don't notice anything else. Time passes, noises go unheard, we don't get hungry, nothing distracts us from the present, which is always the moment of power in our lives.

This is a "state of grace," a very blessed event. Once we've known it, we want to go back to it because all of the chatter and distraction dissolves and we are left with the beauty and power of life fully lived. This can happen just as well when we are vacuuming or doing the dishes as when we are painting a masterpiece. The secret of getting into a "flow state" is to pay complete attention to what you are doing. Stay in the present moment; remember the adage: Be here now.

Simply paying attention to the task at hand is a wonderful form of meditation.

Try it the next time you do the dishes. Feel the warm water on your hands … smell the soap bubbles … see the shine of the plates and cutlery … listen to the sound of the water running and the dishes clinking. Watch your hands and notice the thousands of sophisticated moves they must do well to complete this seemingly mundane task. Much of life goes by unnoticed. This form of meditation asks you to slow down and notice. Immerse yourself in the act of doing the dishes as if it were the most delightful thing you've ever done. Your blood pressure will drop; your breathing will slow down; you will relax.

You can try this mindfulness practice while making a cup of tea, walking the dog or any other simple daily activity.

Exercise and Meditation

In our fitness training program on Maui we incorporate mind-body techniques into all of our movement classes, not just yoga and t'ai chi but also weight training and aerobics. Any form of exercise can be a moving meditation if it is done in the right frame of mind. This means giving the mind something demanding to do to keep it focused. Many of us have been conditioned by an instant gratification culture to have a very short attention span. Our challenge at the school is to keep students involved and aware during all stages of exercise training.

When we are exercising there are two kinds of effective meditation. The first is "association" and it is used during exercise that would be dangerous if we weren't paying attention to our bodies. An example would be someone lifting weights. The instructor's direction would be to "put your mind in your muscle." The participant puts complete attention on the muscle doing the work. We can combine association with visualization. The cue would be "see and feel the muscle growing bigger and stronger." This keeps the person 100 percent involved and makes the workout much more effective.

In the early stages of learning t'ai chi, we use association because the moves are unfamiliar and difficult. We have to pay attention to where each part of our body is in space. Once we have mastered the form, we can abandon ourself to the flow state, or "disassociation" (unless we are practicing t'ai chi as a martial art). Disassociation should only be used in safe situations. For instance, walking or running on a country road and becoming a part of the surrounding nature is safe. Running on city streets with traffic and all the other obstacles around would not be a good time to practice disassociation.

Awareness Walking and Running

Human beings are designed for walking—and running (see Chapter 4 for more information on the importance of gaining aerobic benefits with brisk walking and running to combat PMS symptoms).

The way our bodies are structured is "walking specific." We evolved over thousands of years into the only creature on earth that stands upright, on two legs, as its exclusive mode of self-propulsion. From a mind-body perspective, walking gives us the opportunity to have our head in the sky and our feet on the earth. The opportunities to effect changes on the physical, mental, emotional, and spiritual levels with a structured walking program are profound. This simple act we do every day, when done with direction and purpose, can become a vehicle for deep internal awareness and expanded external awareness.

The swing and swish and rhythms of walking are ancient. They resonate on a cellular level. You relax into an alpha state, blood pressure drops and stress hormones are eliminated by the pumping action of the big muscles in your legs and buttocks. If you add visualization or meditation you increase the benefits of awareness walking tenfold. You can use your walking and running time to actively accomplish goals or to "stop the mind."

Since it is safe to walk every day, you can choose different awareness walking techniques according to your daily needs and desires. You can also adapt these processes to jogging and running as well as using indoor cardio equipment such as treadmills, stair steppers, bicycles or rowing machines.

Be Here Now Walking

This next process has become one of the most popular classes I teach in my workshops all over the world. There are people in dozens of countries practicing awareness walking techniques, so you know you are in good company. Read through this section and the next, "Walk into Your Power," before you go outside or onto a treadmill to try it. You may want to make some reminder notes on index cards to carry in your pocket just in case.

"Be here now" walking is an exercise in present moment awareness or association. As we walk we will shift from a single focus to diffused focus.

1. Begin by being aware of the feel of your heel, ball, and toe as your feet strike the ground. Stay with the rhythm of the heel, ball, and toe, and then bring the awareness up the leg into the hip joint and feel the sensation of your leg swinging freely out to meet the ground. Stay with the swinging; feel the freedom of the swing.

2. Bring your awareness into your breath; feel the breath as it enters and leaves your nostrils. Count your breaths for a few moments. Now notice your arms swinging freely from your shoulders. Stay with the arms for a while and then begin to feel the propelling sensation with the arms and legs swinging in counterpoint.

3. Move your awareness into your torso. Feel your rib cage move with each inhale and exhale. Feel the tilt of your pelvis and notice if the breath creates sensations down into your center.

4. At this point, attempt to hold all of the above sensations in your awareness at the same time. Feel your entire being as a symphony of movement rhythms—feet, legs, breath, arms, rib cage, pelvis. Stay with your body. Continue to bring your awareness back to your body. Your mind will want to wander. You may want to add an internal sound/beat to keep it interested, perhaps count your breaths, or say a cadence (I like to use "I am free, I am here, I am now"), but always bring it back to the physical awareness of the walk and how it feels in your body.

5. Now you are going to let go of all focus and allow your awareness to expand to include everything around you. This is an example of disassociation. See if you can simultaneously feel yourself and your environment without any separations. Let the sounds become you. Feel the air move around you. Notice every rock, tree, cloud, breath, itch, car, dog, breeze, smell, moisture, temperature, person, color . . . all of it. But always include yourself in the picture. Attempt to feel it all as one—no separation. At first this will be very tricky and will require rapidly shifting focus to keep it all in your awareness. After some weeks, as you practice, it will become easier, but it will always require commitment, just as with any meditation.

Walk into Your Power

Another name for this popular walking meditation might be "You Are What You Pretend To Be." By focusing your thoughts as you walk (or run) you are ensuring that you aren't obsessing, in a negative way, about your condition. In this case we will assume the condition is PMS and we will pretend we don't have it. You must be willing to pretend, to role-play. A willing suspension of disbelief is essential in visualization/affirmation work.

In a workshop I led at the Ojai Valley Inn and Spa in California, one of the participants thought this entire exercise was a bit ridiculous. She was a lawyer and very practical. She was also quite overweight and had been for many years. It was a struggle for her to move around so we created her walking visualization as a slender person who could walk for miles without feeling tired. For the first few minutes I could see her resisting and feeling foolish, but I pressed on and kept up the constant flow of verbal, visual and kinesthetic cues about how great she felt in her slender, healthy body.

By the completion of the exercise, she was thrilled. It seems that at some point during the walk, she let go and allowed herself to experience the freedom of feeling the other self that was living inside her large body. The last time she contacted me, she had dropped forty-seven pounds and was still doing her mind-body work.

In this walk into your power exercise, we attempt to engage all of our senses, along with our imagination, to become healthy and PMS-free. The more you practice, combined with the other steps in this book, the more true it will be for you. Use "Walk into Your Power" to imagine any positive change you want to create in your life. Remember, your imagination is the doorway to another world. In this world you already have what you are trying to create—a PMS-free body.

1. Feel as if you are walking in a strong, healthy body that is in peak condition. Imagine how that would feel ... the freedom ... the joy of movement ... no PMS symptoms to intrude in these good feelings.

2. Create a verbal affirmation you can repeat, either silently or out loud, that will reinforce the good feelings. At this time, we are engaging the auditory mode that is most tied in with thought and words. It is important to keep the words positive. For instance, "I love my healthy, PMS-free body. I feel so good today!"

3. See, in your mind's eye, yourself looking just the way you would like to look. See yourself symptom-free, which would mean you would walk lighter, have a much higher energy level, be free from depression and anxiety. See yourself in control of your life, having success with your five-step program.

Visualization

We all use visualization every day. Think about it: when we lie in bed in the morning planning our day, when we fall asleep at night reflecting on what has happened since we woke up, daydreaming, making lists, trying to remember what someone said, thinking about which outfit to wear to the party—all of it is visualization. Human beings are "visualizers," and we have incredible power because of it. There is nothing mysterious or esoteric about visualizing. We use our creativity every day through our thought forms. This section attempts to give you tools to enhance and control this remarkable human talent.

If humans have an estimated 40,000 thoughts a day, for most of us, about 39,990 are repeated, day after day. We dwell in familiarity. This is especially true after we have finished school and have gotten into a groove with work, family, and so on. If it happens that many of those thoughts are negative and worrisome, as they are for many of us, it is adding horribly to our stress levels and aggravating our PMS. Changing our thoughts will change our chemistry. A situation I found myself in during the 1980s is a perfect example of this.

It was a desperate time for me, a time some writers label "the dark night of the soul." My son had gone off to college, my mate of many years left me for another woman, and a business into which I had poured my energy, and the money of friends and family, had failed. I hadn't been able to sleep for more than two or three hours at a time for weeks. As I lay in bed one night obsessing about my predicament and feeling like I was totally alone, broke and over the hill, I knew I had to change the picture quickly or I would get sick.

I knew I needed to feel love and support but I was unable to ask for it in real life because I was so depressed. So I imagined it right then and there in the dark of the night in my bedroom. I created a circle of female ancestors, beginning with my mother and grandmothers and going all the way back to Eve, standing around my bed, holding hands, and sending me waves of love and the knowledge that they were all there for me wanting me to feel supported and relaxed and successful. It worked like magic.

I felt the fear leave, my breathing slow down, the adrenaline stop rushing, the "relaxation response" kicking in, and within minutes I was asleep. I slept well that night and after that, every time I started to go into a negative spin I would immediately begin the visualization I named "support from my female ancestors." If you are a member of a church, you could visualize your support coming from a religious figure. If you feel close to the earth, you could imagine yourself in a forest, nurtured by the surrounding trees. The wonderful thing about visualization is that we can create the way it works best for us.

When using visualizations, the goal is to create an altered state of consciousness. I believe that when we are in a state of deep relaxation, the wall or veil between our conscious and subconscious mind is lowered and we can more easily change deep-seated patterns by inserting new beliefs. First let's get in a relaxed, receptive mode. For that we will use progressive muscle relaxation.

Progressive Muscle Relaxation

1. Choose a warm, comfortable, quiet place. Soothing, instrumental music helps some people relax and visualize.

2. Lie on your back with your palms turned up a comfortable distance from your sides and your feet six to twelve inches apart, falling away from each other.

3. Beginning with your feet, work up the body progressively, tensing and releasing each body part. As you tense, inhale and lift that body part off the floor. As you relax, exhale and release it onto the floor.

4. Begin ... feet ... lower legs ... thighs ... hips/pelvis/buttocks/belly ... chest and shoulders ... back ... arms and hands ... neck/face/head.

5. Complete by tensing the entire body at once, lifting as much as possible off the floor at one time.

6. Release with a big exhale/sigh and breathe normally as you rest or go into a visualization.

Mind Movies

Create a mind movie just like the one we did in awareness walking, engaging your imagination and all of your senses. With your eyes closed, picture a movie screen on the back of your eyelids. See yourself looking and feeling just the way you want to look and feel. See yourself PMS-free, relaxed, happy and successful in your five-step program. This is especially powerful if you have been having trouble with any one of the steps. For instance, if you aren't making the best food choices, see yourself eating correctly to abolish your symptoms. Make your movie as real as possible. Picture the scene, smell and taste the food, hear the accompanying sounds, feel your body in the scene. If you can imagine it, you can be successful doing it.

Make it as real as you can. We see movies in our mind all the time. You are just taking control of them: you are the writer, the producer, the director and the actor. You decide the outcome.

You can create any kind of visualization you want to. For instance, close your eyes and imagine your body surrounded by white light. Picture this light as energy that is healing your body, mind and spirit. When you inhale imagine that you are inhaling the light as health, vitality and relaxation. As you exhale imagine that you are releasing all of your tension, toxins and troubles. Just let them flow out of you on the breath. Use visualization to let go of whatever is not serving you in your life by bringing in its opposite. Always focus on the positive.

Affirmations

When I first begin working with a new personal training client, I give them several three-by-five index cards inscribed with the phrase: "You are an athlete in training." I ask the client to put the cards where they will often see them. Perhaps one on the bathroom mirror, one on the refrigerator door or one on the dashboard of the car. The idea is to remind them that from the day they commit to training, they are to consider themselves an athlete. It doesn't matter what level of athleticism they have acquired, it only matters that they consider themselves an athlete. If they do, they will make the right choices to support the training, such as eating right, getting enough sleep and not missing appointments with me.

Affirmations can be written or verbal, but they must be repeated as often as possible. *An affirmation is simply a goal stated as if it were already accomplished.* It is a constant visual and/or audio reinforcement of that goal. It can be as simple as one word or as complex as a two-page personal mission statement. You can make up your own. Just be sure they are stated positively and in the present tense. For instance, not "My PMS is getting better" but rather, "I am healthy and PMS-free." Here are some other suggestions:

- No matter what happens, I can handle it.
- I am peaceful and calm.
- I attract goodness to me.
- I am confident and relaxed.
- I am grateful for my life.

Music As Meditation

If, as the saying goes, music has the power to sooth the savage beast, it certainly can help relax us. Use music that is soothing to you—perhaps instrumental or nature sounds because often lyrics start our minds thinking. They may remind us of something and we don't want to think. Studies have shown that music has a therapeutic, calming effect on the physical and emotional state. Listen to the music, close your eyes and concentrate on your breathing. Simply relax and let yourself go.

An excellent time to do music therapy is in a warm bath. Use bubbles or aromatherapy salts and candle light. Allow the warmth of the water to ease muscle tension. Focus gently on your breathing and ease into a state of supreme relaxation.

Traditional or Sitting Meditation

This is what most of us think of when someone mentions meditation. We tend to picture someone sitting on a cushion with closed eyes and a straight back. This is, in fact, the form of meditation that creates the profound rest for the brain and nervous system we discussed earlier. Deep states of meditation come when we experience total stillness. To do this successfully, we must follow a few rules.

Suggestions for Successful Meditation

- It is best not to meditate right after a meal. Wait at least an hour.

- For early morning meditations, do a few yoga postures, take a shower or splash some water on your face, to help fully awaken the body and mind.

- A firm cushion or pillow or a folded blanket placed under the buttocks helps to make the sitting more comfortable. Some of you will require a straight-back chair, such as the one pictured on page 36, in alternate nostril breathing.

- Make sure that your clothing is comfortable and sufficiently warm (the body cools down as you relax). Meditate in a well-ventilated room where you will not be disturbed.

- Tend to the process of meditation rather than the goal. Remember that meditation is a science! If you do it properly, you will get the results.

- It's best to meditate in the same place and at the same time every day if you can. Also, if possible, sit facing north or east.

- Two sittings daily of five to ten minutes is a good start for meditation practice. Sit in the morning when you get up and in the evening before retiring. Very early morning (four to seven a.m.) is an especially good time—the atmosphere is very calm, the air clean and the vibrations more conducive to connecting because the clamor of daily life hasn't yet begun.

- Always begin your session with a few yoga postures and pranayama (breathing exercises) to prepare your body for meditation (see pages 31–37). Sometimes it may seem that your mind is more disturbed in meditation than at other times. Usually this is because you've never been still or quiet enough to notice all the "static" on your mental radio. It's all always been there—it's you! Enjoy the "movie"—all the drama, romance, intrigue, comedy—it's all there, in you. Watch the show as it goes by, but don't get caught up in any of the scenes, no matter how dramatic or beautiful.

- Remain as a witness. Use your object of meditation as your anchor. Just keep returning to your practice.

- Practice karma yoga (the yoga of service). Take care of those aspects of your life that cause the mental disturbances. Serve those around you, remembering that the dedicated ever enjoy Supreme Peace.

- Approach your practice with a sense of fun and adventure, but let the mental vision be inward.

- Association with other meditators helps immensely. Join a meditation group if you can.

Choosing a Sitting Practice

I will describe the forms of sitting meditation I am most familiar with and have actually taught to hundreds of students in my trainings in Hawaii and throughout the world. Meditation begins with concentration—trying to focus your mind on any one point. When you are trying to keep your mind on one point whether idea, word or form, you will often see the mind run here and there. Whenever you become aware of it, gently bring the mind back to the point. In another few minutes (or seconds!), it will run to another idea; bring it back.

There is a saying in the Hindu tradition, "The mind is a drunken monkey." Our assignment is to learn to focus it. This constant effort of bringing the mind back again and again to the point is what we call concentration. In yoga the Sanskrit word for concentration is *dharana.* When the concentration of the mind is lengthened, you are approaching meditation. But don't think you are wasting your time when your mind is not fully concentrated. No one has achieved meditation immediately upon trying.

Pranayama, or breath awareness, is covered earlier in this chapter. This is one of the most important mind-body techniques available to us and should be used as preparation for any other type of meditation you practice.

Mantra, or sound, meditation, is the type that corresponds to TM and Herbert Benson's relaxation response. Choose a word that has a positive meaning for you and repeat it internally. For example, the sacred syllable *om,* used in the yoga tradition, seems to set up a vibration in the brain that is soothing. If you aren't comfortable with that, try the word *home.* It has the same effect and is more familiar. Just be careful it doesn't set your mind off and running … home … home … oh, yeah, I forgot to call Mom … gee, did I take out the garbage?… the grass is getting so long—when does the gardener come again?

... You get the idea. When you notice your mind wandering, gently return it to the mantra.

In traditional meditation a mantra must be a sacred word. Perhaps you might want to use the word "God" or "love." I often teach my students to use the word *one*. It suggests a joining with a higher power and, when repeated internally, has a nice vibration. Breathe normally, without thinking about it.

Vipassana, or mindfulness meditation, instructs us to simply watch our breath as it enters and leaves our nostrils. Focusing on the breath is one of the most profound forms of meditation. Breathe naturally. Thoughts will intrude; simply observe them come and go without getting attached to any particular one. Let them float by as if you were watching a movie. The goal is eventually to realize that you are not your thoughts or even the events of your life. You are eternal.

Visual object focus can be done with the eyes open or closed. I prefer teaching this with closed eyes, but you may want to try it both ways and see what works for you. Look at or imagine a candle flame, a flower or a religious symbol, something that you can use to refocus your mind any time it wanders. Imagine that you are dissolving and becoming one with the object of your meditation. Breathe normally, without thinking about it.

As you sink deeper and deeper into meditation—with any of these sitting practices—detach from your thoughts, and become one with your focus point, your breathing will slow way down and be so gentle it will seem to practically disappear. Congratulations! You have joined the ranks of practiced meditators and will reap the benefits for the rest of your life.

Yoga

When I first began my mind-body trainings in Hawaii in 1980, yoga was still considered something strange and exotic by most of America. The fact that we included it, along with t'ai chi and meditation, in our professional training programs kept us from being accepted into mainstream fitness for many years. It wasn't until the mid-1990s that fitness conventions would even allow these mind-body arts to be presented as professional workshops.

We have come a long way. Well over 1,500 studies have been done on yoga, including research in 1992 demonstrating that yoga does not need to be aerobic in order to decrease anxiety and anger and improve mood. Yoga is now recognized as one of the most effective exercise regimens for health and longevity. The strength, flexibility and peace of mind gained through this discipline become obvious to anyone who does it regularly for a few months.

Yoga is now available in nearly every health club, spa, and YMCA and YWCA in the country. Yoga studios are springing up everywhere. People have discovered yoga and it is changing their lives. For those of you still unfamiliar with this wonderful healing art, I will give you a little background. Since yoga is a vast body of knowledge with many different "arms" or approaches, it is necessary to limit our information to the basics that will have the most immediate effect on PMS.

Yoga is a Sanskrit word, and its most common interpretations are yoke or union. Proper execution of the yoga exercises we will learn requires focusing a great deal of attention on the body and the breath with the ultimate goal being a union of body, breath, mind, emotion and spirit. When this coming together occurs, even somewhat, a sense of inner balance is restored.

Combine this sense of inner balance with the physical benefits of yoga and you are well on your way to renewed health and a feeling of well being. In her book *Healing Mind, Healthy Woman,* Alice D. Domar, Ph.D., director of Women's Health Programs at Harvard Medical School's Division of Behavioral Medicine, reports, "Many of my patients with widely varying women's conditions find yoga to be an enormously valuable and effective way to relax, release tensions, reconnect with their bodies and relieve symptoms."

The practice of hatha yoga, or the yoga of postures, involves three basic components. We've already covered the components of breathing, called pranayama, and of meditation. This section is specific to the physical poses called asanas. These poses have been a written tradition for about 1,000 years. The belief amongst yoga scholars is that yoga philosophy had been an oral tradition for thousands of years before that.

The fact that any exercise form survives for hundreds of years indicates to me that it works! And probably works very well. As a fitness specialist, who teaches everything from aerobics and weight training to yoga and t'ai chi, I ask myself, will "step aerobics" still be around and evolving in 1,000 years? Probably not. Yoga is a very sophisticated system that becomes a way of life for the long-time practitioner.

One of the most profound discoveries I made at the Strong, Stretched & Centered training was that I could reduce and even eliminate PMS and menstrual pain through yoga, meditation and deep relaxation. I found that I could control my discomfort and gain a feeling of total well-being and acceptance of the changes in my body. I have a much deeper understanding of my body. I continue my own practice and teach to other women the importance of mind-body fitness for achieving freedom from PMS without medication. It is a gift to build one's own strength through the powers of mind-body fitness.

—Debra Dimancesco, United Nations, Geneva, Switzerland

Yoga Your PMS Away

Yoga postures release the tension in our muscles and, even more important, relax and tone the nervous system. The exercises improve posture, increase blood and lymph circulation, strengthen joints and boost the immune system. One of the main reasons yoga is so effective for easing PMS is because the postures help regulate the endocrine system.

The endocrine system is the source of our hormones. It is a series of ductless glands that secrete their chemicals (i.e., hormones) directly into the blood and lymph systems. It is the function of these hormones to keep our metabolism balanced. This is an incredibly complex interaction that basically regulates most of what goes on in our body and mind. The endocrine system mediates the mind-body link. Hormones intensify emotions, and powerful emotions upset the complex interrelationships of the hormones. Yoga creates balance in the endocrine system. It gives us a degree of control over this powerful system.

The Iyengar and Viniyoga Methods

Within the hatha yoga tradition there are several styles. The exercises we present are derived from two well respected in the West today, Iyengar and Viniyoga. In these exercises, you will either stretch into and hold postures while practicing deep breathing or move in and out of postures gently, several times, linking the breath with the cycles of movement.

Many yoga postures are beneficial for PMS in that they contribute to a strong, stretched and centered body and mind. The ones I have selected are specific for relief of PMS. During your session, pay attention to your breath, your alignment and your state of mind. When your attention starts to wander, use the breath to bring it back. Remember, yoga means union. It is also recommended to use "beginner's mind" when practicing yoga.

Each time you do your mind-body routine, do it as if you have never done it before. Bring a state of complete attention and do not assume you have anything figured out. This allows for spontaneity, and each time you practice you have the opportunity of learning something new about yourself. It also will save you from expectations. If you are using beginner's mind, you will never worry about doing as much as last time. Your body is different every day. Don't compete with yourself or anyone else.

For simplicity's sake we will not use Sanskrit names for the postures. We will also not include a yoga warm-up because for PMS it is ideal to use the t'ai chi exercises for the warm-up. Our goal is to incorporate the most useful variety of mind-body exercises for PMS into a reasonable amount of practice time.

Choose a private space that's warm and quiet, if possible. Wear loose, comfortable clothing, preferably cotton. In addition, find a comfortable mat or rug that will not slide under you and will contribute some padding. It's best to wait two hours after eating before you practice yoga. If that's not realistic, wait at least one hour and make sure the meal is small.

A Yoga Series for PMS

Half Tortoise with Cat Stretch

1. Begin on your hands and knees with your knees directly under your hips, your hands directly under shoulders.

2. Inhale as you lift your chin and tailbone up and relax your middle into a sway back.

3. Exhale as you arch like an angry cat, lifting your navel and dropping your chin and tailbone

4. Still exhaling, gently lower your hips onto your feet into the half tortoise stretch (feel the stretch from your fingertips all the way back through your hips; pull your shoulders away from your ears).

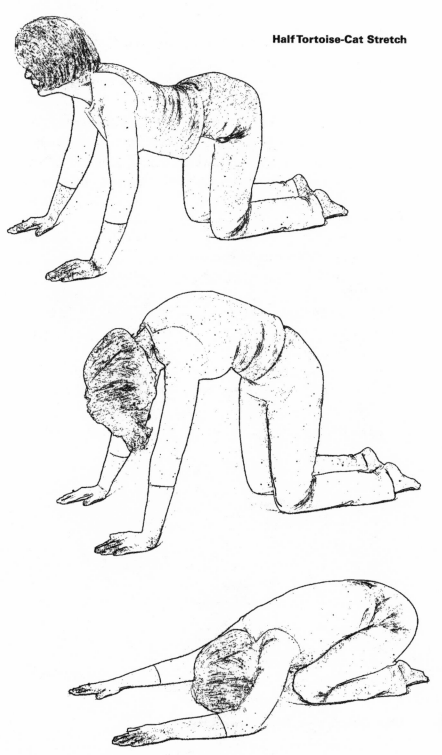

Half Tortoise-Cat Stretch

59

5. Inhale again as you lift back onto your hands and knees and relax into the sway back.

6. Repeat three times moving slowly and attempting to make the breath last as long as the movement.

Benefits: Limbers and relaxes the spine and brings circulation to the pelvic region. Relieves congestion and improves functioning of the organs in the pelvic region which aids digestion and elimination. Increases strength and flexibility of the arms and shoulders.

Spinal Twist

If you have a spinal disc problem be very cautious with this exercise or consult with your physician.

1. Lie on your back with your arms flat on the mat at shoulder level.

2. Bend your knees and gently lower them to your right side.

3. Turn your head toward the left as if you were trying to get your ear to the mat.

4. Each time you exhale, feel your body relaxing deeper into the pose. Hold for several breaths and then do the other side.

Benefits: Improves circulation to, and limbers the shoulders,

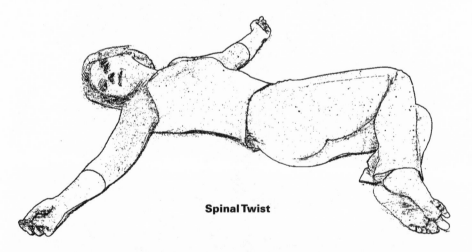

Spinal Twist

back and hip joints. Relieves congestion and tension in the pelvic region and improves functioning of the internal organs. Aids digestion and elimination.

Diamond Pose

1. Sit with a straight back, the soles of your feet together, grasping your feet with your hands, your knees relaxed toward the floor. In the beginning it may help to use a pillow like we did in seated meditation. Move and breathe slowly.
2. Inhale deeply.
3. As you exhale slowly, lean toward your feet while pushing gently on your thighs with your elbows.
4. Inhale as you gently return to the straight back position.
5. Repeat three times and then relax as far forward as you can and hold for a few deep breaths.

Benefits: Limbers the lower back, hips and groin muscles. Relieves congestion in the pelvic region and tension in the back and inner thighs.

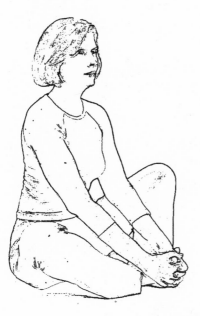

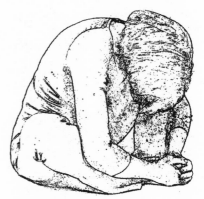

Diamond Pose

The Bridge

This exercise can be done as either a static pose or a repetitive cycle.

1. Lie on your back, bend your knees and bring your feet as close to your hips as you can comfortably.

2. Place your feet about hip width. Allow your arms to relax by your sides with your palms down.

3. As you inhale, lift your tailbone and roll up through your spine, vertebra by vertebra. While you are doing this slow roll-up, pull your tailbone toward your legs so your spine is elongated. Keep your shoulders on the floor and allow your back to arch until you feel a stretch in the front of the body

The Bridge

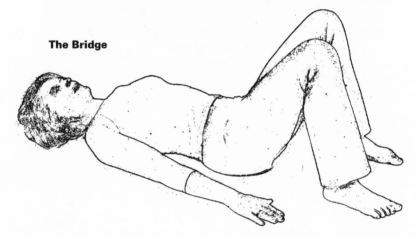

but are not uncomfortable. Keep your chin tucked toward your chest.

4. If you are doing the holding posture, stay in this position for at least three deep breaths.

5. Next, on an exhale, roll down vertebra by vertebra.

6. If you are doing the repetitive cycle, do three slow rollups and downs, always inhaling on the up and exhaling on the down. Try it different ways on different days.

Benefits: Stretches and releases tension from the front of the body. Strengthens the back of the body. Improves functioning of the thyroid and increases circulation to the head.

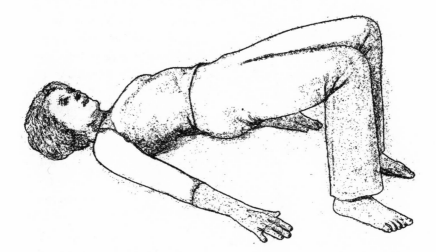

Knee Pump

This exercise has the very important job of stretching out the low back after the intensity of the bridge exercise.

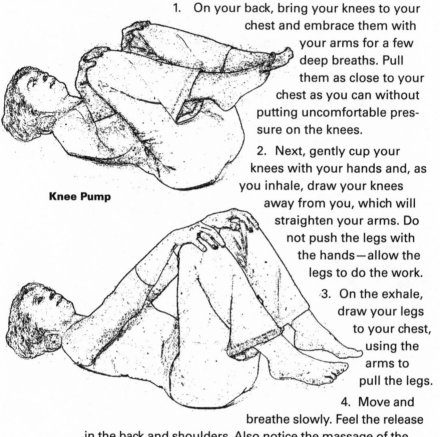

Knee Pump

1. On your back, bring your knees to your chest and embrace them with your arms for a few deep breaths. Pull them as close to your chest as you can without putting uncomfortable pressure on the knees.

2. Next, gently cup your knees with your hands and, as you inhale, draw your knees away from you, which will straighten your arms. Do not push the legs with the hands—allow the legs to do the work.

3. On the exhale, draw your legs to your chest, using the arms to pull the legs.

4. Move and breathe slowly. Feel the release in the back and shoulders. Also notice the massage of the pelvic organs.

Benefits: Increases circulation and relieves congestion in the pelvic region, including the low back. Stretches the low back. Aids digestion and elimination.

Hamstring Stretch

1. Lie on your back with your knees relaxed as close to your chest as they will go.

2. Inhale and as you exhale straighten your legs and press your feet toward the ceiling. Never allow your legs to go past a ninety-degree angle with your hips. This could put a strain on your low back. If your legs won't straighten in this position, just extend them as far as you can. The hamstrings will loosen up in time. Do the excercise one leg at a time if your hamstrings are very tight.

3. Exhale as you draw your knees back to your chest.

4. Do three full cycles, and on the fourth extension hold your legs in the air for a few deep breaths. Each time you exhale feel the hamstrings in the back of your legs releasing more tension. If this movement is easy for you, do it with your feet flexed (toes pulled toward body) for additional stretch.

Hamstring Stretch

Benefits: Stretches and releases tension from the legs, hips and low back. Massages and increases circulation to the abdominal organs. Reduces swelling and fluid retention in the legs and ankles.

The Hindi Squat

This is a difficult position, but if you do it carefully, in time, it becomes not only easy but actually a comfortable way to sit. We all did it as children—it was natural. If you have knee or hip joint problems, proceed cautiously. Ideally your weight should be dropped back into the hips not over the knees. This protects the knees.

1. Stand with your feet parallel to each other, about ten to fifteen inches apart.

2. Begin by holding on to the back of a chair (with someone or something weighting it down) and lowering yourself slowly to the floor. If you don't have anyone to weight your chair, try hanging on to a doorknob. The important thing is that you have something to hold that will support your body weight.

3. Sit back and down as far as possible. At first you may end up on your toes. That's okay. Stay in the position as close to ideal as you can attain without too much discomfort, and do a few deep breaths. As your hips, knees and ankles become more flexible, your heels will come down. Remember, your weight should be centered in the pelvic area, not over your knees.

4. Eventually you will be able to let go of your support, your buttocks will be just a few

inches off the floor and your legs will open to allow your elbows to come to the inside of your knees. At this point, press your elbows against your knees, with your palms together and straighten your back. Ideally your feet should stay parallel, but in the beginning it might be easier for you to allow them to turn out a bit. Just be sure you track your knees over your feet so they are in alignment.

5. Hold the position, at whatever level you are capable of, for four to ten deep breaths.

6. Rise slowly out of the posture on an exhale, using your support if necessary.

Benefits: Increases flexibility in the low back, hips, calves and ankles. Increases strength in legs and hips. Aids digestion and elimination. Relieves congestion in the pelvis which helps eliminate discomfort from PMS and menstruation.

After completing this exercise, repeat the hamstring stretch to release the tension that builds up in the hamstrings during the squat. Don't skip this, it's very important!

Hindi Squat

Step 1: Treat Your Whole Self **67**

The Butterfly

Be sure you keep your low back pressed into the floor. This exercise 'may cause a bioenergetic release, which can cause trembling in the legs and pelvis. This is a good thing. Allow it to happen. It eliminates tension in the pelvic floor.

1. Lie on your back with the soles of your feet together and your knees in a relaxed, open position; inhale.

2. As you exhale, slowly close your legs one-third of the way. Hold the position while you slowly inhale.

3. Exhale as you slowly close your legs another one-third of the way. Hold the position while you slowly inhale.

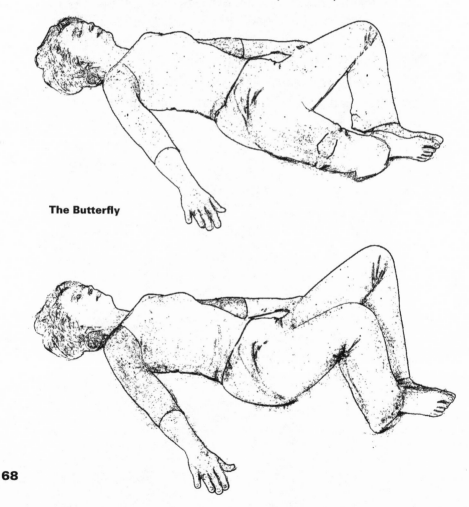

The Butterfly

4. Exhale as you slowly close your legs the final one-third of the way, allowing the soles of your feet to come flat to the mat.

5. Inhale and open your legs naturally, bringing the soles of the feet back together.

6. Repeat the cycle four to six times.

Benefits: Increases circulation to and energizes the entire pelvic area. One of the best for PMS relief.

After completing this exercise, repeat the knee pump exercise to stretch your low back.

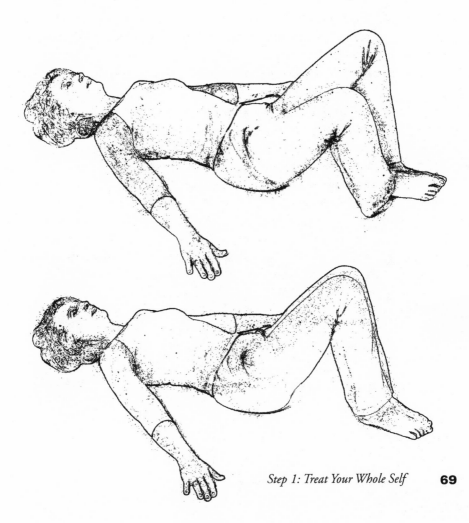

Now we are finished with the exercises and it is time to rest. Choose one of the following relaxation postures to complete your sequence. It is advisable to do relaxation with supports when you have no time constraints and can continue in a relaxed frame of mind even after your mind-body practice is done.

Deep Relaxation Posture

1. Lie on your back, either flat or with a pillow under your knees if it feels better for your lower back.

2. Rest your arms a comfortable distance from your body, palms up.

3. Place your feet about twelve inches apart and allow them to fall away from each other. This will release any tension from the legs.

4. Rest in this posture and breathe easily and naturally for two to three minutes.

5. Allow your mind, body and spirit to profoundly relax. If you find thoughts intruding, it helps to do the healing light meditation (page 49). When you are ready, turn on your side and push yourself up with your arms.

6. Sit on a cushion or chair and go directly into pranayama and meditation.

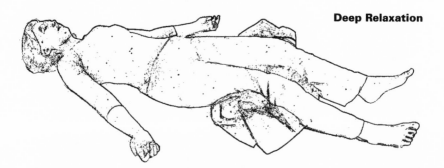

Deep Relaxation

Deep Relaxation with Supports

This posture is derived from the practice of restorative yoga and should be done when you have between three and ten minutes to rest and breathe on the props. The purpose of this posture is to allow yourself complete surrender in your body, mind and spirit. By supporting yourself with the props, you will feel safe and nurtured. You can allow softness in the belly and opening in the chest while relaxing the lower back. You can find the props around your house. In the illustrations, blanket rolls are used to support the arms. Throw pillows support the knees so there isn't any strain on the sacroiliac joint.

Remember, this posture is to relax the abdomen and open the chest, not to stretch the thighs. Bed pillows support the back with an extra throw pillow under the head in the first position. In the second position, the extra pillow is removed so the head is level with the torso. Try it both ways and see which is more comfortable for you.

Keep in mind, the purpose is complete relaxation. In both positions, your forehead should be higher than your chin. If you can't keep your feet from sliding away from your body, do the pose with a wall as a prop.

**Deep Relaxation
with Supports**

1. Arrange your pillows and blankets so your feet will be right up against the wall to prevent movement. You can also cross your ankles; just be sure you change the bottom ankle to the top halfway through your time, to balance the stretch. If you feel any strain in your back or chest, reduce the height of the back support. If you feel strain in your hip joints, increase the height of the knee supports.

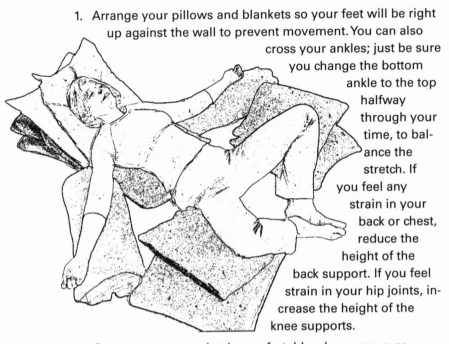

2. Once you are completely comfortable, close your eyes (some students like to use an eye bag or cool cucumber slices on the eyes to relax them), and breathe easily and naturally. Do not practice deep breathing in this pose. The point here is to do nothing.

3. Travel with your mind through your body and feel each part relaxing beginning with the toes and finishing with the throat, jaw, face and scalp. Imagine you can feel your body healing from all the stresses of life. Feel your body relaxing into health and vitality, opening to goodness, surrendering to peace.

4. After three to ten minutes, take a few deep breaths and turn on your side.

5. Lie for a couple of minutes in a loose fetal position and then push yourself up with your arms. Sit on one of the cushions (or a chair) and go directly into pranayama and meditation.

T'ai Chi Ch'uan

Upon observing my first t'ai chi class, back in the early 1970s, I was immediately impacted by the gracefulness of the movements. I watched for a long time and realized that it was the circular flow of the dance that captured my attention and made it seem so flawless—almost magical. T'ai chi, more than any other exercise form I've studied, has the effect of stopping time and releasing me into the moment.

When I began the practice of t'ai chi, it quickly became apparent that the easy grace I had observed was both difficult to achieve and, later, once achieved, a way of circulating healing energy in the body. Our first t'ai chi instructor in the Strong, Stretched & Centered program on Maui, Bruce Turnbull, taught that t'ai chi was a beautiful dance, a moving meditation, and a martial art. In our training programs, we use it as a way to slow down and really begin to feel movement, and therefore life, coming from our own center of being. This center is, literally, considered to be a couple of inches below your navel and in the middle of your pelvis. On a practical level, we use t'ai chi to develop strength, flexibility, coordination and cardiovascular efficiency. The result of combining all of these traits is an integration of mind, body and spirit.

Dating from tenth-century China, t'ai chi has developed as a unique blend of healing art and martial art. Since coming to the United States in the mid-1960s, t'ai chi has emphasized its healing art aspect, primarily because of the importance placed on relaxation, which in the West we call "stress reduction." The Qigong Bibliographic Database, developed by the nonprofit Qigong Institute, cites 1,300 qigong studies done on qigong (also called Chi Kung) and t'ai chi since 1986 in China, the United States, and Europe. T'ai chi has been shown in a number of these studies to improve psychological well-being, as well as to provide a wide variety of other health-enhancing benefits.

In this section, we will emphasize the therapeutic nature of t'ai chi, and its usefulness as a self-discovery tool. This approach is designed for maximum relief of PMS.

Go With the Flow

T'ai chi practitioners believe that doing the form keeps the chi flowing freely and unblocked throughout the body, especially to the organs. In Chinese philosophy, chi is the life force, or vital energy, that is different from measurable, physical energy. This is the same force that is defined as prana in yoga.

Imagine the stress and tension in your body as a hose knotted in various places. As the water, or chi, tries to pulse through the hose, the knots slow it down at times to a mere drip. Removing the knotted areas allows the full force of water to come coursing through; all of our body is nourished.

Another way of understanding this concept is through acupuncture. The movements of t'ai chi are designed to stretch and release (open and close) the meridians used in acupuncture. Meridians are the invisible lines along which the acupuncture points are arranged and the chi flows. Blockage in these points is what is believed to cause illness. Acupuncture needles are used to unblock specific points so the chi can flow freely. Acupuncture is also commonly used for pain relief. Stimulating the points releases endorphins—our natural morphine—in our brain. The opening and closing movements of t'ai chi ch'uan are a kind of self-massage for the acupuncture points leading to healthy energy (chi) flow, long life and vitality.

The Basics

Ron Perfetti, president of the Hawaii T'ai Chi Ch'uan Association and current t'ai chi instructor for the Strong, Stretched & Centered training program teaches that all of the benefits outlined above are the outcome of the mastery of five t'ai chi movement principles:

- Centering. This involves placing the attention two inches below the navel and in the center of the pelvis. Centering represents the true movement/balance center of the body.
- Relaxation. Through relaxation, we eliminate the habit of accumulating tension and tightness that hinders the body's ability to move with ease and strength.
- Rootedness. This principle represents our understanding of our relationship to the earth as well as our sense of moving from the ground up to maximize stability, confidence and strength.
- Posture. Good posture in t'ai chi is the study of, and sensitivity to, how we position and move the body in respect to gravity, from the feet up to the head.
- Single weightedness. Also known as "shifting of weight," this principle is often the most difficult to grasp. Partially it means having all of the weight centered over one leg at a time while the other remains weightless and ready to move in any direction. It also means how we shift or transfer the weight from one leg to another.

"These principles should not so much be viewed as separate qualities but rather as parts of a whole, which results in what t'ai chi has traditionally called 'effortless strength,' " says Perfetti.

Movement As Metaphor

To add mindfulness and a spiritual aspect to t'ai chi, we simply consider how each of the principles of movement can be used to interpret how we live our lives. This is very powerful and requires honesty. If you are inspired with a different interpretation of a t'ai chi principle for your life, by all means, use that. Inspiring awareness is one of our main goals with t'ai chi.

Centering asks that we live our lives from our own source of power. This principle says that no one has control but us, it comes from deep inside and expands outward, and we only need to understand that to step into our power. This is important for PMS because much of our stress is a direct result of our feelings of powerlessness.

Relaxation in our mind and spirit allows us to trust that we have help in our lives, and even though we are in control, it's also safe to "let down" and ask for what we need. That may be something as simple as a favor from a friend to take some of the load off or as profound as trusting in a higher power. When I am overwhelmed I remind myself that I have help from my spiritual source. This has been stated as "let go and let God." I am never alone and this fills me with great peace. When we relax the knots of doubt in our mind and spirit, the waters of creativity flood our being. This is fabulous for PMS because one of the big problems for women today is feeling like we have to "do it all."

Rootedness as a metaphor asks that we reflect on how we relate to our place in the world, on our planet. When we feel rooted, we have the sense of connection and belonging of a giant Sequoia that has been growing for hundreds of years. Rootedness is our "ground connection," our ability to move on the earth and accomplish our goals. Feeling rooted helps alleviate the sense of alienation and frustration so common in the world today.

Posture is truth in presentation. Are we sensitive to the impact we have on others? Are we getting the results we want as we move through the world? Are we connected and balanced between earth energy and spiritual energy? Are we moving through life with a sense of dignity and pride balanced by humbleness and service? When we are able to answer yes to these questions, we will have developed peace of mind. Stress and peace cannot exist in the same mind, heart or body.

Single weightedness represents our ability to live 100 percent in the present moment. Learning to slow down our movements and feel our bodies exactly where they are corresponds to inhabiting our lives fully in the present moment. Also, through "shifting of weight," we begin to realize how often we are ahead of ourselves, or back there in the past somewhere ... anywhere but here. When we practice the "empty step" of the t'ai chi walk, we begin to understand the power of commitment: the commitment to being fully aware, awake and alive right now.

A T'ai Chi Ch'uan Practice for PMS

Notice that every t'ai chi principle—centering, relaxation, rootedness, posture and shifting of weight—is inherent in the following series of simple exercises designed to alleviate PMS symptoms. Even though these exercises are described in stages they should be practiced as continuous, flowing movements. "Basic stance" will be utilized for each of the exercises, so you will want to practice it first. Basic stance is represented in the first illustration of the waterfall hands exercise (pages 80–81).

To perform basic stance:

1. Stand with your feet parallel on the outside edges, between hip and shoulder width, arms relaxed at your sides.

2. Keep your ankles straight.

3. Bend your knees slightly.

4. Stay in erect posture with your pelvis over your ankles, your rib cage over your pelvis, and your head over your shoulders.

5. Don't allow your body to lean to the back or the front.

6. Imagine that you have a straight line drawn down the side of your body, through the middle of your ear, middle of your shoulder, middle of your hip, just behind your knee, and middle of your ankle.

7. Relax your shoulders.

8. Please keep your eyes on the horizon for all t'ai chi practice. Resist the tendency to look down.

Turning from Center

1. Begin in basic stance and keep your knees slightly bent throughout this entire exercise.

2. Slowly shift all of your weight to your right leg, creating a body position where one leg is completely full and the other leg is completely empty.

3. Simultaneously, you are turning your pelvis (center) to the left as far as the hip joint will allow.

4. Feel as if you are sitting down on your right leg but don't allow your body to go out of alignment.

5. Slowly shift all of your weight to your left leg as you turn your center to the right as far as your hip joint will allow.

6. Continue to slowly shift and turn, making certain that one leg is full and one leg is empty. Imagine that your legs are full of sand and that, as you shift your center over your right leg, the sand is slowly pouring out of the left leg into the right. This is easy and flowing: the "sand" should pour from left to right and right to left, like an egg timer.

7. When you are very comfortable with this, allow your arms to relax as if they were wet noodles. As you become proficient at "turning from center," you can move more quickly. If you are really loose and relaxed in your arms and shoulders, your arms will naturally flop around your body as they do in the exercise illustration. Don't move your arms; let them go, and eventually they will move of their own accord. It's as if weights were tied to your hands.

8. Breathe easily and naturally.

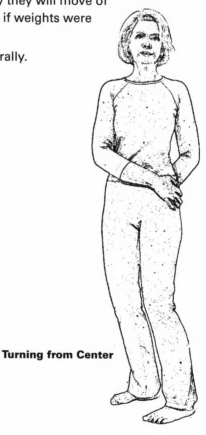

Turning from Center

Waterfall Hands

1. Begin in basic stance but turn your palms to the back.

2. Inhale slowly and allow your arms and hands to float up to shoulder level as if they were floating up on the breath. It is a totally relaxed move—you should feel no tension in your neck, shoulders or arms. The visualization that t'ai chi masters use is "beautiful ladies' hands." This implies total relaxation of the joints but with energy, chi ... not limp or lifeless.

3. Your knees are simultaneously, slightly straightening. T'ai chi masters insist the movement of the arms only happens from "center," not from muscle action in the arms and shoulders. The arms move because the chi is moving. This is quite advanced, but we can begin now to imagine or visualize what that would feel like: "effortless strength."

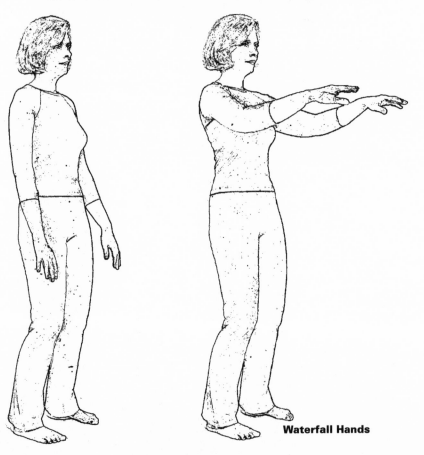

Waterfall Hands

4. Exhale slowly as you allow your elbows to release toward your sides. This will draw the hands toward the shoulders.

5. Continue to exhale as you release your upper arms next to your sides. Your hands will slide back and down (wrists bent back) toward your chest, as if over a waterfall, and lower to the beginning position. Your knees are simultaneously releasing to the beginning position during the entire exhale.

6. Inhale and begin again. Move slowly and make the inhale and exhale last as long as the movements. Repeat several times until you feel a tingling energy in your hands when you stop. Close your eyes ... be still ... breathe and allow a feeling of peacefulness to fill you.

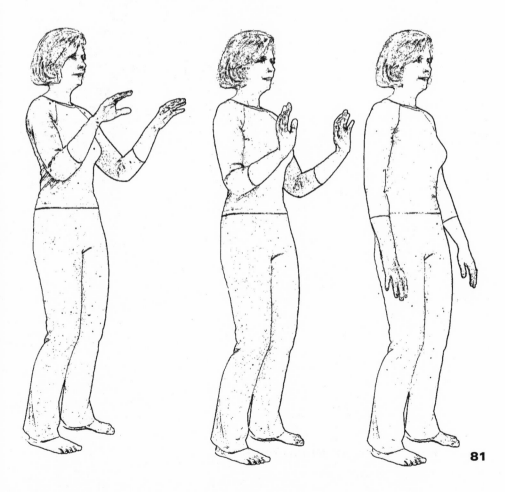

Icon King Breathing Exercise

Some t'ai chi teachers call this the "Tibetan Longevity Exercise." The monks in Tibet are said to do this 100 times a day. With that many repetitions, it becomes an upper-body aerobic exercise and would certainly contribute to longevity. Do this exercise as effortlessly as possible. Visualize the movements coming from the gentle lifting and lowering of your center and the inhaling and exhaling of your breath. Pay special attention to keeping the shoulders dropped and relaxed. This is a wonderful breathing exercise. It helps deepen vital capacity and also links the breath with the body.

Icon King

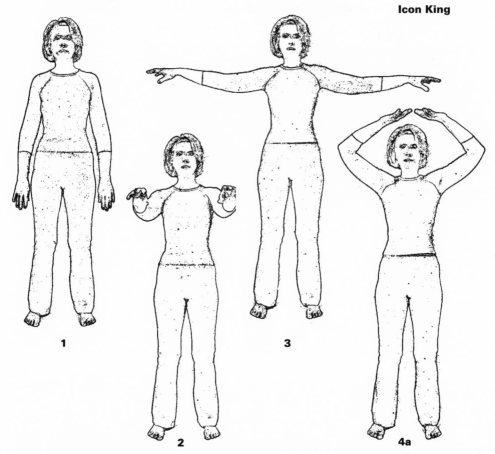

1

2

3

4a

1. Begin in basic stance and turn your palms to the back.

2. As you inhale, press down with your feet, straightening your knees, raising your arms to shoulder height, wrists relaxing.

3. As you exhale, release the leg press, allowing a slight bend of the knees, and open your arms out to the side, simultaneously drawing your shoulder blades together.

4. As you inhale, press down with your feet, straightening the knees and raising your hands, first over the head with palms turned up and fingertips barely touching, and then into a slight stretch up above the head. This is a long inhale.

Icon King

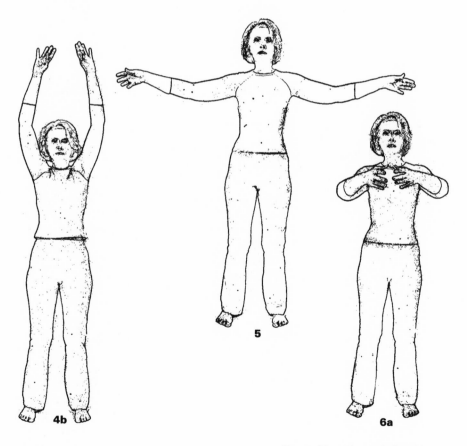

4b

5

6a

5. As you exhale, release the leg press, bending the knees, and lower your arms to shoulder height at your sides, palms front, there letting the wrists relax.

6. As you inhale, press down with your feet, rising slightly, and bring your hands first forward in front of your body, making a diamond shape with your thumbs and index fingers, and then toward your face. It's as if you are scooping the air into your nose.

7. As you exhale, release the leg press, bending the knees, and gently press your hands, still in their diamond shape, down the front of the body. When they have dropped as far as they will go, release them back to beginning position.

8. Repeat this exercise three to five times at first. As you gain endurance in the upper body, increase to six to ten times.

Icon King

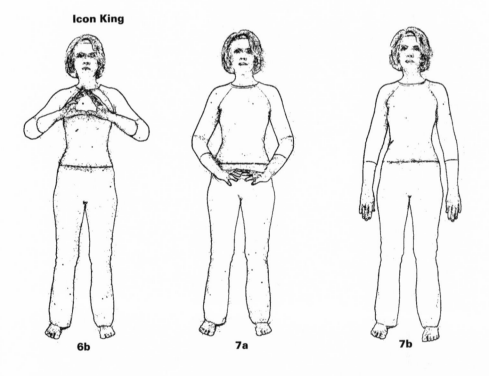

6b   7a   7b

T'ai Chi Walk

1. Begin in basic stance.

2. Inhale, and as you exhale, sink 100 percent of your weight onto your left leg. (For the duration of this exercise the knees are slightly bent. When you are doing the t'ai chi walk, you are in an even plane—there's no rising and falling of the body. This is a great workout for the legs.) Simultaneously allow your forearms to lift slightly, palms down. The arms maintain this position during the entire t'ai chi walk. Remember your erect posture and relaxed body. Your right leg is completely "empty."

3. Inhale as you lift your right foot and place it shoulder width an easy step in front of you. Maintain parallel feet. It's as if you were t'ai chi walking on railroad ties.

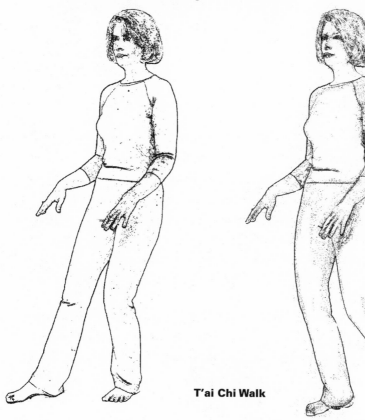

T'ai Chi Walk

4. Only step as far as you can without shifting any weight to the right foot. Your weight is still 100 percent on your left leg.

5. Exhale as you slowly shift 100 percent of your weight to your right leg until your left is completely "empty." Just your toes of your left foot will remain on the floor, but there will be no weight on them.

6. Inhale as you lift your left foot and place it shoulder width an easy, parallel step in front of you.

7. Continue this slow shifting of weight as you inhale and exhale for a couple of minutes, at least. When you lift your back foot and place it in front of you for your next step, imagine that you are setting it down on eggshells. It must be a very soft, empty foot until you actually begin the transfer of weight. This is a very powerful walking meditation and will captivate you once you have mastered it. It takes a great deal of willpower not to lose concentration. Stay in the present moment.

Pilates

Unlike our other mind-body practices, this one is the inspirational and visionary work of one man. Joseph Pilates lived from 1881 to 1967. When he died at age eighty-six, his method was very popular with a small segment of the population. When he lived in New York and was around professional dancers and athletes, it became obvious to him that injuries were common—more common than he thought they should be. He decided that, with his understanding of the body, he could do something to correct this situation.

Pilates had been a gymnast, boxer, circus performer and fitness trainer. He was very educated regarding optimal and efficient use of the muscles for the performance of specific movements. He set out to create a method of training that would build a strong body

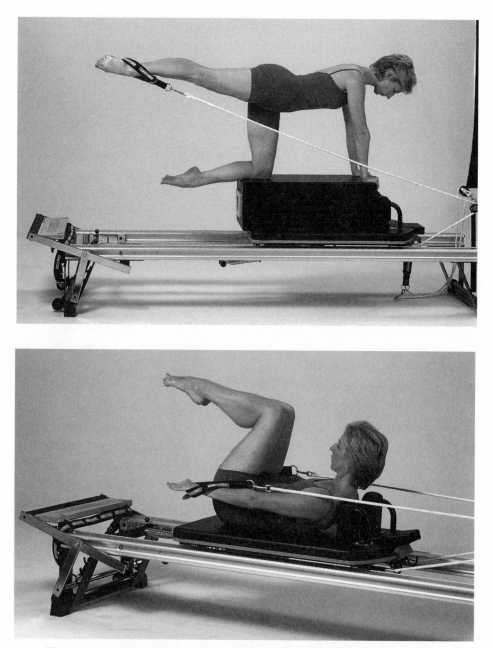

Pilates extension and contraction exercises done by Moira Stott on a Stott Professional Reformer.

that could move freely, without unnecessary strain on the muscles and joints. He initially called his technique "contrology," and described it as "the science and art of coordinated body-mind-spirit development through natural movements under strict control of the will. Contrology movements are designed to exercise to its full extension every single bundle in the 800 voluntary muscle-motors each of us has been given to alter ourselves."

Pilates Principles

One of the main principles of Pilates® is that of enhancing core stabilization to create coordination, balance, agility, and joint stability. Learning to initiate our movements from our core, or our center, allows the extremities (limbs) to move freely on a stable spine. This is a similar concept to "moving from center" in t'ai chi. Relying on core muscles not only improves movement technique, it also creates an elongated, lean, lithe look. Maintaining a strong center is advantageous to any physical movement, including everyday activity.

The Pilates method is clearly a combination of Eastern and Western philosophies. The technique is a reflection of Pilates' life experience—the German sense of precision and order (he was a native of Germany), merged with the Spartan pursuit of physical strength. The Pilates method also reveals an understanding of Eastern mind-body disciplines, such as yoga and t'ai chi. The movements are slow and exact, requiring mental concentration and proper breathing technique. Enthusiasts report feeling peaceful, yet energized from the work, while having strengthened their muscles on the deepest level.

How It's Done

Pilates is a system of controlled strengthening and stretching exercises done most commonly with a piece of equipment called a "Reformer" that involves a sliding bed with springs to provide resistance and nylon cords to control movement. Other equipment includes the trapeze table, barrels, discs and more. The user sits, stands, kneels or reclines—and the variations are endless (hence, the nickname, "jungle gym for adults.")

As we mentioned, the primary focus of the exercises is on strengthening core abdominals, pelvic muscles and the torso. Instead of working on muscle groups one at a time, Pilates (as well as most mind-body exercises) trains the body as it works in real life: in smooth, integrated movements that involve a number of muscle groups simultaneously. Pilates works deeper muscles than are commonly accessed through traditional weight training workouts, and provides active stretching through a full range of motion.

Hospitals and clinics from Germany to Italy to numerous sites in the United States use Pilates for orthopedic, neurologic and chronic pain conditions. The number of physical therapists using Pilates-based methods continues to grow. Therapeutic Pilates is often reimbursed by insurance (when referred by an orthopedist or physician for physical therapy). Although it may take two to three months to see rehabilitation results, dramatic improvements in posture, pain and body awareness are often seen in just a few sessions.

Benefits for PMS

According to Sean P. Gallagher in his book *The Pilates Method of Body Conditioning,* "the exercises stimulate the circulatory system, oxygenating the blood, aiding lymphatic drainage and releasing endorphins which are responsible for the 'feelgood' factor. The immune system is given a boost to provide greater resistance to disease and illness." Training in proper body mechanics in a gravity reduced setting (sitting or lying) on specially designed equipment can even alleviate muscular imbalances resulting from something as extreme as scoliosis and leg length discrepancies.

A training program begins with small range of motion skills.

As these are mastered, you learn how to incorporate them into larger movements, often with resistance on the Pilates equipment. At this point, correct breathing becomes an important part of the training. Finally you learn to apply these principles to actual movements used in your dance, sport or daily activity.

This is a unique program, and although there are Pilates mat classes, maximum benefit is gained when working on the special equipment Joseph Pilates designed. Look for a Pilates studio near you. There are Pilates trainers in many clubs and spas, and the number is growing. With the modern, portable Reformer equipment, qualified Pilates trainers can now conveniently come to your home.

Step 2: Find the Fitness/Freedom Connection

GLORIA KEELING

I admit it—I hate exercise. I know it's supposed to be good for you, and good for PMS, but who wants to exercise when you feel fat, irritable and depressed? What I really want to do is go to bed with a gallon of chocolate ice cream—not go to a gym and parade around in front of a bunch of skinny, cheerful fitness fanatics!
—Heather, accountant, Joliet, Illinois

WHO DOESN'T KNOW THAT EXERCISE is good for you? Yet it can be one of the most difficult things to fit into your schedule—especially when PMS is sapping your energy and enthusiasm.

Many women think of exercise as one more obligation to try and squeeze into their day. Translation: one more thing to feel guilty about not doing. It's a vicious circle—PMS makes you feel too fatigued and stressed-out to exercise, then it magnifies your guilt over not exercising enough!

Is there any way out? Yes! Research has shown that exercise is a highly effective way to alleviate PMS symptoms. Dr. Kallins has had outstanding results with patients who have started and maintained a regular aerobic exercise program, just as I have seen many, many women take charge of their health and defeat PMS with a lasting commitment to an active lifestyle.

How did they do it? By throwing out any negative old stereotypes of exercise and freeing themselves to create a positive new relationship with physical activity that fits their personal interests, abilities, goals and schedule. Dr. Kallins and I call this the *fitness/freedom connection.* It means that instead of associating exercise with duty or guilt, you begin to link it with a new freedom to become active in the ways that work best for you, connect with your body's natural talent for movement, take care of yourself— and have fun doing it.

Where do you begin? Commit these three new fitness freedom principles to memory:

1. "Aerobic exercise is one of the best tools I have to free myself from PMS, reduce stress, improve mood and help my overall health."

2. "I don't have to do any particular exercise just because someone else does or the way someone else does it—I can get active my own way and find what works best for me."

3. "I am going to give myself the gift of a regular aerobic activity program because my mind and body need it—and I deserve it."

If you are already doing aerobic exercise, you know how great it feels to be active. For you this will be a refresher course to strengthen your commitment. If you aren't doing aerobic exercise, this information is essential to becoming PMS-free.

What Is "Aerobic"?

This may seem like a very basic question, but the truth is that you will have a much easier time starting or sticking to an aerobic exercise program if you have a very clear idea of what it is and how it works magic on your health.

Your cardiorespiratory system includes your heart, lungs and vascular system (arteries, veins and capillaries). A simple definition of the word aerobic is "with oxygen." This just means that you exercise at a pace that your body can sustain without getting out of breath and becoming oxygen deprived.

Exercise of Choice for the Heart

Your heart is a muscle that beats (contracts) an average of 100,000 times a day, or more than 36 million times a year. It moves five quarts of blood in your body through 60,000 miles of blood vessels. Over the next twelve months, your heart will pump 730,000 gallons of blood—that's about twenty-eight swimming pools' worth. Your heart has to work very hard, and you can help it tremendously by doing aerobic exercise.

As your heart muscle contracts, it sends blood to the lungs to pick up oxygen and then out to the body to deliver that oxygen. The amount of blood your heart can hold is called *heart volume.* The amount of blood your heart pumps with each contraction is called *stroke volume.* Your heart is just like any other muscle in your body: if you exercise it, it becomes bigger and stronger, and can hold more blood and pump more with each contraction.

Regular aerobic exercise enables the lungs to successfully pull more oxygen out of the air you breathe. Your lungs become very efficient at extracting oxygen, which then attaches to some of your 25 trillion red blood cells, goes back to the heart and is pumped out to your body. All the extra oxygen and nutrients in the blood wouldn't mean much if your body couldn't use them at the delivery end. This is where the muscles you have been exercising become more efficient.

When you exercise your muscles aerobically, they need a consistent flow of oxygen delivered to them. The blood flows out from the heart in arteries, then branches out into the capillaries which are so small the oxygen and nutrients can pass through their walls into the cells easily. After delivering its load, the blood picks up the waste products produced by cell metabolism and carries them away, via capillaries, and then through the veins, for disposal through either the lungs (our exhale) or organs, such as the liver and kidneys.

When you exercise aerobically, your muscles grow more capillary beds. This is called *increased capillary density.* It makes the delivery and disposal system to and from your cells so much more efficient. Your cells also become better at metabolism—they are able to use the energy provided by the oxygen and nutrients more efficiently. And actually, you increase the amount of blood in your body. This is called blood volume. The more blood, the better your entire energy delivery and waste disposal flow can work.

Which Exercises Are Aerobic?

When I was an aerobic dance instructor during the 1970s and 1980s, we used to call aerobic exercise "LSD" for "long, slow, distance." This means that you exercise at a slow enough pace that you can maintain it for time and distance. Instead of bursts of intense energy output such as in sprinting, basketball, volleyball, tennis or other stop-and-go sports, you work at a constant level that is determined by your age and existing state of fitness.

The most efficient way for your body to get aerobic is to work the large muscles of the lower body, because they make a big oxygen demand when exercising. Examples of aerobic exercise are aerobic dance, walking briskly, jogging, running, biking, indoor stationary cycling, rowing, cross-country skiing and swimming. It's also possible to stay aerobic when working with weights if you do circuit training, in which you move quickly from one exercise to another with stops in between to do brisk movements that keep your heart rate elevated.

The Magic of Aerobic Exercise

Aerobic exercise has an incredible list of benefits. At one time, most research on the benefits of exercise was done on men, but results from relatively recent studies done on women show that aerobic exercise is also beneficial for health concerns that are specific to women, such as breast cancer, osteoporosis and even menopausal hot flashes.

Decreased body fat is one of aerobic exercise's most popular benefits. Recent studies have shown that regular exercise can sometimes be more effective than dieting and is one of the most consistent predictors of successful weight management—meaning that if you exercise regularly, you're more likely to succeed at reaching and staying at a healthy weight. Dr. Kallins points out that, among its other benefits, aerobic exercise:

- Reduces blood pressure.
- Decreases total cholesterol.
- Increases HDL cholesterol (the "good" cholesterol), which helps protect against heart disease.
- Helps control blood sugar and, therefore, diabetes and hypoglycemia.
- Elevates endorphin levels, believed to be associated with decreasing anxiety, tension and depression.
- Releases the build-up of toxic stress hormones.
- Improves posture, coordination and agility.
- Increases flexibility and musculoskeletal strength.
- Improves concentration levels, self-image and personal satisfaction. (Women have time for themselves when exercising—so often our lives are focused on taking care of others.)
- Improves sleep patterns.
- Increases self-esteem. (We are proud to display our fit, healthy bodies.)

Come up with a few benefits of your own, such as rediscovering your old love of sports or more opportunities to play with your children or dog. For me, a big one is getting outside to do my awareness walking. I am so thankful I have an excuse to be outdoors in the fresh air every day.

Benefits of Aerobic Exercise for PMS

Your body is one integrated unit working as a whole, and all of the benefits of exercise will impact your experience of PMS. However, these two aspects of aerobic exercise are believed by Dr. Kallins and many other experts to specifically address PMS symptoms:

1. Aerobic exercise affects your body's metabolism of glucose. When your body digests carbohydrates, it breaks them down into the simple sugar glucose, which your cells (and their mitochondria) use for energy. As glucose enters your bloodstream, the pancreas releases insulin, a hormone that helps the cells use the glucose. Levels of insulin and glucose fluctuate throughout the day, depending on when and what you have eaten. When your blood sugar is low, you may feel nervous, tired and anxious. Low blood sugar also produces the food cravings that are so common in PMS.

Aerobic exercise helps to stabilize blood sugar levels, because it calls on muscles to release stored energy into the bloodstream. If you find yourself craving sweets or experiencing late-afternoon crankiness, twenty or thirty minutes of aerobic activity will make you feel a lot better than indulging in a chocolate bar. The candy will send your blood sugar skyrocketing, but it will soon drop, leaving you wanting something else to eat. The exercise will steady your blood sugar, and you'll be able to make better decisions about what to eat for dinner. The effect that aerobic exercise has on blood sugar alone is very important in managing the symptoms of premenstrual syndrome.

2. Aerobic exercise raises the body's level of endorphins and other chemicals produced in the brain. These are our natural opiates ("feel good" hormones), and they are responsible for the well-known "runner's high." Some experts have theorized that endorphin levels fall during the premenstrual period, leading to anxiety and depression. Exercise can help bring these levels back.

How Often and How Hard?

Exercise produces specific health and fitness benefits based on how much you do and how hard you train. Research is still confirming the precise amounts and types of exercise needed to achieve specific types of benefits. However, we know more than we ever have about how to use physical activity to improve our health physically, mentally, emotionally and even spiritually.

The American College of Sports Medicine (ACSM) suggests that to achieve most of the general health benefits available from physical activity, you should exercise moderately for about thirty minutes most days of the week. This can include utilitarian, or "lifestyle," exercise, such as vigorous gardening or walking briskly up and down stairs or through the mall. Recent research has also shown that these health-enhancing bouts of daily exercise can be broken into smaller, separate chunks, such as ten minutes of activity done three times each day.

What Is Energy Metabolism?

In your cells are tiny organelles called mitochondria. They are like little sausage-shaped cells within the cell. These organelles are where your energy is actually produced from glucose, where calories are turned into energy. There are mitochondria in all of your cells, but the muscle cells have the most because muscles need the most energy.

When you exercise consistently, you not only increase the numbers of mitochondria in your cells but the ones you have actually get bigger and more efficient. There you have it: one of the secrets to why exercise creates both weight loss and increases in energy.

It is extremely important for every woman to realize that even a little bit of activity is better than none—and every little bit counts. The worst thing you can do is tell yourself that if you can't formally and regularly work out at the gym, any activity is a waste of time. Any amount of activity is never a waste of time when it comes to your health.

You should also know that the more you train physically (up to the point of overtraining or exercising for several or more hours each day, where exercise becomes detrimental to your health), the more health and fitness benefits you will realize. While even a little exercise is far better than none, more exercise is generally better for you than less.

Exercise benefits expert Ralph La Forge, M.S., suggests that for a balanced program of activity that will win you optimal health benefits (physically, mentally and emotionally), you should strive to do:

In our Western culture, we usually stop dancing once we've passed the singles club scene stage. How sad for us. It keeps us young to dance, not just our bodies but also, and above all, our spirits. Rediscovering dance is one of the reasons aerobic dance classes became so popular during the 1970s and 1980s, and ethnic and club-style dancing are re-emerging again today.

Join a class if you want to, but you can do it in your living room, too. Dancing with wild abandon has a marvelous effect on our beings: we get to pick the music, be the choreographer, and create the dance just for ourselves.

Whatever physical activity you choose, I hope you enjoy it with the same passion and creative energy that I find when I dance. Make your choice of physical activity your own personal "dance" of celebration. Dance for yourself. Dance for your life. Dance for sheer joy.

- Regular aerobic exercise three times a week.
- Utilitarian exercise such as household chores or yard work four to seven times a week.
- Resistance training twice a week.
- Mindful exercise such as t'ai chi or meditation walking several times each week.

Of course, these can be combined with each other in creative ways to best fit your schedule.

Your PMS Aerobics Prescription

Exercising aerobically several times a week is of primary importance for PMS-free living. These traditional "F.I.T.T." principles provide good guidelines for you to plan your beginning aerobics prescription for PMS-free living:

Frequency: *How often should you exercise?* For your PMS aerobics prescription, it is safe to begin with three to five times a week.

Intensity: *How hard should you exercise?* To determine this, use the target heart rate (THR) guidelines that follow.

Time (or duration): *How long should you exercise?* For your needs as a beginner, twenty to thirty minutes at your THR is adequate. The ACSM states that beyond thirty minutes, the increase in musculoskeletal injuries outweighs the increased aerobic benefits for beginners.

Type (or mode): *What kind of exercise should you do?* It is extremely important that you choose an aerobic exercise that is appropriate to your health status, likes and dislikes, time availability, equipment and facilities availability. You may find that you love indoor stationary cycling, a particular step training or martial arts-based video or vigorous hiking on a trail near you. Whatever you do, don't feel pressured to do a form of exercise that really doesn't appeal to you. Remember, the important thing is to stick with an active lifestyle, not just start one. You may also need to try a variety of activities to find the one(s) you enjoy the most.

Choose any activity that uses large muscle groups (legs) and can be maintained continuously and is rhythmical in nature. If you are not accustomed to regular exercise, a good way to begin is with walking. Walking at a brisk pace will raise your heart rate and give you aerobic benefits. It requires no special equipment, other than suitable shoes, and doesn't stress your joints as running does. You can use the time more efficiently if you also do the visualization, "Walk Into Your Power."

If you are already active, or are young and healthy, you may need to try a more strenuous form of exercise, such as stair climbing or running, to achieve aerobic benefits. What form of aerobic exercise you use will ultimately be up to you. Here are a few tips for staying active rather than dropping out:

- It helps to have a workout partner. If you know a friend is counting on you to meet them for a walk, you are much less likely to drop out.

- Another key to exercise adherence is cross training. Walk one day, swim another, bike another . . . this prevents boredom and is also better for your body. It helps prevent the overuse injuries that can happen when you repeat the same moves day after day.

- Be prepared for your activity habits to change. As you become more fit, you may find that new activities appeal to you (you may advance from walking to running, for example), or a schedule or location change may make a different activity more practical. Be flexible, but never, ever deny yourself the benefits of regular physical activity.

Achieving Your Target Heart Rate

After you have been doing aerobic exercise for some time, you will know instinctively when you are working exactly hard enough to get the benefits we have been discussing. In the beginning, however, you need to know how to take your pulse and figure out if you are in your THR range. This is not difficult—it just requires a little math. I recommend using a calculator. It takes all the guesswork out of the process. The formula looks like this:

1. Subtract your age from 220.
2. Multiply the answer by 60 to 80 percent. Which percentage you use depends upon how fit you already are.
3. Multiply the answer by 1.15.

Here's how it works:
- Susan is thirty-five years old and fairly fit, so we will use 70 percent in her formula: 220 − 35 = 185 x 70% = 129.50 x 1.15 = 148.93 (150). When Susan takes her pulse during aerobics (we'll explain how to do this in the next section), she should have a heart rate of 150 beats a minute.

- Jane is thirty years old, but she is overweight and had a

baby recently so we will start her at 60 percent of her maximum heart rate: 220 – 30 = 190 x 60% = 114 x 1.15 = 131.10.
When Jane takes her pulse during aerobics she should have
a heart rate of 131 beats a minute.

- Carole is twenty years old and was very active in high
school sports so she is still in really good shape. We can use
80 percent in her formula because she is both fit and young:
220 – 20 = 200 x 80% = 160 x 1.15 = 184. When Carole takes
her pulse during aerobics, she should have a heart rate of
184 beats a minute.

There are many factors that affect heart rate. If humidity is
high or you are exercising at altitude, your heart rate will be
faster. It will also be faster if you are tired or sick. Medications of
all kinds affect heart rate. Some send it higher and some lower, so
you need to check with your physician or pharmacist.

It's important not to exceed these guidelines; don't overexert
yourself when you are first beginning. Remember LSD: long,
slow, distance. If you overexert, you may get discouraged and
quit. Keep our small do-able steps in mind.

Taking Your Pulse

Digital heart rate monitors are popular today, and Dr. Kallins has
had great success using them with patients. A heart rate monitor
is worn on your body, and it gives a readout of your heart rate at
any given time. You may want to consider using a heart rate monitor to help your activity program—if so, just make sure you get
one that is simple enough for you to understand and use correctly.

It's also a good idea to know how to take your own pulse. It's
simple. There are four sites that are recommended; find the one
that works best for you. (Never use your thumb for taking a pulse
because it has a pulse of its own and that can be confusing).

1. **Apical site:** Place the heel of your right hand on your chest, over your heart.

2. **Carotid site:** Place the index and middle fingers of either hand on the side of your neck, midway between your ear and your chin.

3. **Radial site:** Place the index and middle fingers of either hand on the inside thumb edge of the opposite wrist.

4. **Temporal site:** Place the index and middle fingers of either hand on the same side temple.

Once you have found your pulse, observe the second hand on your watch or clock. Take your pulse for ten seconds and multiply by six. So, if you count twenty-two beats in ten seconds, your heart rate is 132. If you count thirty beats your heart rate is 180.

Practice taking your pulse when you are not exercising. Become familiar with it. Record your resting pulse. What is your pulse when you are sitting around watching TV or reading? Put this in your journal because after a few weeks of consistent exercise, your resting pulse will be lower (your heart muscle is getting stronger).

During exercise, stop and take your pulse about every ten minutes until you get a feel for how hard you need to work to be at your target heart rate. Try to keep your legs moving in place while you take your pulse to prevent blood pooling in your legs.

One quick way to know if you've gone above your THR is the simple talk test. Can you carry on a conversation while you're doing your aerobics? If you can't, you are no longer aerobic. You shouldn't get out of breath, so slow down your pace.

Warm-Up and Cool-Down

To warm up for your aerobic exercise, do the activity at a low level of exertion for a few minutes. Even a brief warm-up activates the enzymes in your body that help manufacture aerobic energy. Your body is more efficient. Warming up also prepares the joints and muscles to help prevent injury. If you are going to walk on the treadmill at 3.5 miles per hour, start for three to five minutes at 2.5 miles per hour. Cool down in the same way: three to five minutes of steadily lowering intensity until it is down to 2 miles per hour. This means that if you want to get twenty minutes of aerobic exercise, you have to do thirty minutes of activity to allow for warm-up and cool-down time. If you want thirty minutes of aerobic exercise, you must do forty minutes of activity.

Your body will be eternally grateful if you also take a couple of minutes to do these three stretches for your legs after your aerobic workout.

1. Stand near a wall and place the ball of one foot against the wall with your heel on the floor and the leg straight. Hold and press your body gently toward the wall. This will stretch your calf and Achilles tendon. Hold for twenty to thirty seconds and then do the other leg.

2. Hold on to the back of a chair or a counter—something for balance. Stand on your left leg, pull your right foot behind you, lift and hold it with your right hand. Feel the stretch in the front of your right thigh. Hold for twenty to thirty seconds, change, and do the left leg.

3. Sit on the forward edge of a hard chair or bench. Straighten your right leg and place that heel on the floor with your toes pulled toward your body. Bend the left knee into a ninety-degree angle with your foot flat on the floor, then lean toward that leg with your upper body. This is a hamstring stretch for the back of the right thigh. Hold for twenty to thirty seconds and change legs.

Strength and Flexibility

Although we've been talking primarily about aerobic exercise, since it has been shown to have the most positive impact on PMS, you should know that your body also needs strength and flexibility to stay healthy.

Strength training, or working with weights, is excellent for many reasons. One of the main ones for women is maintaining bone density, which counteracts the loss of bone mass that occurs with age. Aerobic weight-bearing exercises such as running and dance will slow bone loss, but weight-training will actually build bone mass. Osteoporosis, the loss of bone that is common in women after menopause, is preventable in many women with weight-bearing exercise that works against gravity, as well as adopting healthy eating patterns and taking nutritional supplements.

Flexibility, or stretching, is also necessary for your body to stay young, supple and injury-free. Make sure that you know the right kinds of stretches to complement your favorite aerobic activities. Yoga can be an excellent way to maintain and improve your flexibility. A personal trainer, fitness instructor, physical therapist or yoga instructor can help you plan a flexibility program to fit your lifestyle.

Law of 10,000 Steps

We are members of the animal kingdom, and animals that aren't allowed to move get lethargic, depressed, obese, sick, even psychotic. Nothing works well when animals are confined, so why are we surprised when our self-imposed confinement contributes to problems such as those related to PMS?

It is not natural to be sedentary, and yet our culture gets more and more sedentary every year. To be healthy, ideally we need to walk (or run or climb) about 10,000 steps a day (this falls under the utilitarian or lifestyle category of exercise but can also be part of your aerobics prescription if you're running, walking or hiking briskly enough). Many people are surprised to find they walk as little as 2,000 to 3,000 steps a day. That's dangerously low.

I recently walked to the store which is 0.9 miles each way, or just under 2 miles round-trip. It took me 2,400 steps. (I actually counted!) That means I have to be on the move for approximately 8 miles a day to get in my 10,000 steps. Some of those steps need to be in the THR, but a lot of them don't. They just have to add up to around 10,000.

I tell my clients to stand up during TV commercials and step in place. You can march, you can step side to side, or walk in circles around the couch. Count your steps. Brisk marching in place is about 100 steps a minute. If you march for six minutes of commercials each hour for three hours of TV watching, you will have stepped 1,800 steps toward a healthy body, simply by getting up off the couch during commercials!

In my house/office I have one phone, and it's on a short cord. If it rings or I need to make a call, I have to walk to the phone. I probably knock out about 400 to 500 steps a day just doing phone calls.

When you're doing errands, park the car away from the store and force yourself to walk or use the stairs instead of the escalator or elevator. If you work in an office, take five minutes of every hour to walk briskly, even if it's just up and down the hall. Are you concerned about what your co-workers will think? Just tell them it's doctor's orders. Movement is our birthright and we need to claim it.

Designing Your Personal PMS Workout

By now you're wondering how to start—what's most important and how to fit it into your busy life. We have presented two aspects of fitness: mind-body techniques and aerobic training recommendations. Both of these are equally important for establishing freedom from PMS. You will want to build up to working three days a week with your choice of aerobic exercise and three days a week with your mind-body routine. In the beginning it would be optimal if they can be on different days: perhaps M-W-F for aerobics and T-Th-S for mind-body. The sessions don't have to be long at first, just consistent.

If that's not possible, arrange it whichever way you can. It's more important to do it than to fret about how you split up your days. For instance, if you must do them at the same time on the same day, attempt to get your aerobic exercise first and follow it with a mind-body session for your cool-down. If you can split them between morning and evening, aerobics are a great way to energize at the start of the day and t'ai chi and yoga are perfect for unwinding at the end of the day.

Let's take a look at a four-part plan of direction and motivation to begin your fitness program for PMS-free living.

1. Create Your Own Aerobics Plan. If you haven't been exercising at all, begin with an easy ten- to twenty-minute walk on your aerobic days. If you are choosing to join a gym, use whatever aerobic equipment you enjoy. You may want to try one of the many aerobic dance, step or other kinds of classes available. If you choose to run, read at least one of the excellent books for beginning runners. *Runners World* magazine is also a helpful resource.

If you live where you can't walk outside or get to a gym, remember the option of music and dancing or simply marching in place while you watch TV. There are also excellent videos for beginning and advanced workouts, and everything in between.

Whatever you choose, be sure you are working in your target heart range by either using a heart rate monitor or taking your pulse. As soon as you start to feel fit, and this brief aerobic workout is easy for you, begin to add time to your routine and increase the number of days you do it. How far you take this is up to you. Once you start aerobic exercise and see how good it is for you and how terrific you feel, you can never tell what might happen. You could end up in a marathon!

Try to increase to forty minutes, including warm-up and cool-down time, as quickly as is safe for you. Some research indicates that to get the most benefit from aerobic exercise, you should burn 2,000 calories a week. For a person who walks briskly, that is six hours of exercise; for a runner, three. While this may be optimal, both Dr. Kallins and I have seen many, many women realize great relief from PMS symptoms with less.

2. Create Your Own Mind-Body Plan. The complete t'ai chi section, yoga section, five minutes of pranayama and five minutes of meditation described in Chapter 3 will take thirty to forty minutes, depending on how long you practice each exercise.

If you don't have much time, choose the exercises that feel best to you. Consider learning them all so you will have each at your disposal when you need or want them. Your ten-minute mind-body workout might look like this: the t'ai chi exercise "Turning from Center" for warm-up, followed by the yoga postures "Half Tortoise with Cat Stretch" for your back and shoulders, the "Hamstring Stretch" for your legs, "The Butterfly" for your pelvic floor, and ending with a few seated diaphragmatic breaths and one minute of meditation.

Something every day will help to relieve tension and pain as well as other PMS symptoms. For optimum relief, I recommend three days of the entire routine (thirty to forty minutes) and four days of a ten-minute routine during your symptomatic days.

3. Set Your Priorities. At this point it's normal to start wondering how you are going to fit this all in. Life is already busy enough. However, there are 168 hours in a week. If you sleep seven hours a night (recommended!), that leaves you 119 hours. If you exercise six hours a week, that's only 5 percent of your waking hours. HELLO! That's not a lot to ask in exchange for a healthy, fit, relaxed body. It shouldn't even be an issue.

If you have four kids and a full-time job, it will be more difficult but just as important. You need time for yourself, time for your body, time for your spirit. Do a thirty-minute walk on your lunch hour and a mind-body routine just before going to sleep.

4. Use Your Self-Discovery Journal. The Chinese philosopher Lao-tzu once said, "The journey of a thousand miles begins with a single step." This book is your first step onto a path that leads to a different way of living. Hopefully this path will increase your pleasure in life. It certainly has for me, my students, and Dr. Kallins' patients.

If you honestly do your five-step program, and do it consistently over time, you will change a lot. Some of the changes will be fast and very noticeable, some will be subtle, gradual and perhaps even outside your conscious awareness. This is why it's so important to write every day, even for a couple of minutes, in your self-discovery journal. Don't underrate this part of the process.

How you feel, how your thoughts are changing, how your body is changing, the new understanding and awareness that you have, all of these are the result of your five steps to a PMS-free life. In a year, you will be quite glad you took the time to record these changes while they were happening.

5 Step 3:
Eat to Beat PMS

GEORGE J. KALLINS, M.D.

ARE YOU READY TO LOOK AT FOOD from a whole new
perspective? I advise my patients who struggle with PMS
to stop thinking of food as a source of comfort, a means
of survival or the fulfillment of a particular craving—and to start
treating food as a powerful weapon for managing their health,
including PMS.

There certainly is no lack of food theories and eating schemes
these days. However, I've found that all this conflicting information can cause doubt, confusion and some rather unusual eating
behaviors. Some of my patients tell me they "eat lots of meat
again, now that they know protein is all that really matters," or
that they get most of their vitamins and minerals from "diet
shakes and energy bars." Unfortunately, many of these eating
plans lack the most important ingredient of all: balance.

Healthy living is a matter of balance, and so is healthy eating.
Going to extremes in any area of life undoubtedly causes strain in
other areas. Too much of anything, even a good thing, can be
damaging. Balance is a goal worth striving for in all areas of life,
and I've found it to be an invaluable ally in the fight against PMS.
Everything you eat has a unique impact on your body. Your hormones respond in different ways to different foods as they are digested and enter your bloodstream. Since PMS is very likely
related to hormonal imbalances, it makes sense that your food

choices can work for you or against you as you try to manage your symptoms.

PMS is not only associated with hormonal imbalances but also with blood sugar fluctuations and deficiencies of vitamins and other nutrients. It is well within your power to erase or decrease many symptoms of PMS by making informed, thoughtful food choices to bring your body back into balance.

How should you begin? With an open mind—because healthy eating, and in particular, eating to beat PMS—may require a significant shift in your lifestyle and how you think about food.

A Lifetime Plan

We know that eating habits are one of the most difficult behaviors for many people to change. In spite of the tremendous amount of information available about healthy eating, obesity and other health problems related to diet continue to grow. It would be a mistake to pretend that changing dietary habits is simple.

However, I know from my experience with patients that changes in eating habits are possible to make, especially when you're motivated to overcome an obstacle like PMS. The secret? Here are the five principles I've discovered from women who have succeeded in developing new balanced eating habits—and defeating PMS:

1. Be realistic. You're probably not going to give up all your favorite foods overnight. But I've had patients who didn't think they had any willpower who gave up nearly all refined sugar in their diets. They didn't necessarily do it on the first try, or even the second. But over time, as they made small, gradual improvements, the dramatic changes in how they felt spurred them to make changes they never dreamed possible.

2. Pleasure is important. This is crucial to remember because you don't want to set yourself up for an eating plan that you'll end up sabotaging. It is possible to eat healthfully *and* pleasurably. You probably already have some healthy food choices you enjoy, and there are many more to discover, if you're willing to find them.

3. Find what works for you. Individuals vary widely in how they respond to different foods and in specific nutrient needs. It often takes time to develop trust in your body's reactions to diet, but the more you practice by introducing gradual change and paying attention to how your body reacts, the more you'll discover about yourself and your ideal eating plan.

4. Try new alternatives. The only way you'll ever find the best eating program is to try a variety of options. You may think that a vegetarian diet would never satisfy you, that you could never get used to tofu or that increasing your protein couldn't make much of a difference in how you feel. Leave your preconceptions behind and take a chance. What finally works may be the one thing you were sure wouldn't.

5. Don't give up! I've noticed that people sometimes get so frustrated with conflicting information on food or the challenges of making changes that they surrender altogether. Resist the temptation to give up. Dietary changes can make an enormous difference in your monthly experience of PMS, your health and your overall enjoyment of life.

Relieve PMS with Ten Dietary Changes

The following ten dietary tips would be a lot to swallow at one time. Instead, choose several to start with, and gradually add in the rest. I have included action steps to give you a start. Maintaining the ones that work is up to you.

1. Switch to mini meals. One simple diet change you can make is to balance the amount of food you eat each day. Instead of the traditional three square meals, I advise eating at least six smaller meals throughout the day. Eating a mini meal every two hours is a good rule of thumb to follow because this will help maintain a steady blood sugar level, which can help prevent mood swings.

Action Step: Try eating mini meals for one week and write about your experience in your journal of self-discovery. If you find it difficult, plan your mini meals in advance so you don't skip them.

2. Consider going 40-30-30. I have found that many of my patients have had success in relieving PMS symptoms with a 40-30-30 diet, where 40 percent of their caloric intake came from protein, 30 percent from carbohydrates and 30 percent from fat. This is the eating approach introduced by Barry Sears, Ph.D., in his best-selling book, *Enter the Zone,* and it has certainly garnered its share of controversy.

Although a diet in the range of 50 to 60 percent carbohydrates, 10 to 20 percent protein and 20 to 30 percent fat is more commonly recommended by nutritionists and health organizations, I believe it's important for every individual to experiment—to find what fits best.

Some of my clients have found that the proportional increase in protein and decrease in carbohydrates has improved their mood, weight and energy level. Others have found it unsatisfying or difficult to maintain. The important thing is for you to try new alternatives and get in the habit of monitoring your response to new ways of eating. Then, when you find what works, *stick with it!*

Action Step: Keep a food diary for one week to see what percentage of protein, carbohydrates and fat you are eating. Then plan to adjust these percentages during the next week. Again, planning your foods in advance may help you manage better.

3. Pay attention to protein quality. Protein is not something you can do without. It is in charge of cell growth, immune system functioning and fluid regulation. Proteins are made up of essential amino acids. Your body cannot manufacture these itself, so it must rely on your diet to supply them.

A lot of attention has been paid to the amount of protein you eat, but the real focus should be on the *quality* of the protein you choose. The four best sources of proteins for women trying to control PMS symptoms are fish (oily, saltwater fish is best; avoid freshwater fish because of possible contaminants), soy products (tofu, tempeh, miso, soy nuts, soy powder), egg whites, and legumes.

Research has shown that women who consume a low-fat vegetarian diet have blood estrogen levels that are two to three times lower than those who eat a high-fat, meat and dairy-centered diet. Lower levels of estrogen may translate into a decrease in the symptoms of PMS.

If you are an avid meat or chicken eater, cut back to once or twice a week and select only lean cuts of beef and skinless poultry. Switch to low-fat or, preferably, nonfat dairy products and use only the whites of eggs.

Action Step: Chart your protein intake for one week. Is it coming more from high-fat sources or the PMS-beating sources listed? Plan to substitute better sources in the week ahead.

4. Make more soy choices. When your mother told you to eat your beans, she probably wasn't referring to soybeans. In fact, in days gone by, the soybean was simply not found in most American kitchens. Little did we know that this centuries old staple of the Asian diet would rise to "soy stardom" at the end of the twentieth century in the United States. And this is one bean with staying power.

Not only does its humble form pack more protein-punch than

many of its legume counterparts, it may also single-handedly have the wherewithal to treat a whole host of serious health problems, including PMS.

We all remember the Four Food Groups from our grammar school years and the colorful pictures of red meats, yellow cheeses and frothy white milk in sparkling glass containers. In the United States, the land of plenty, a healthy diet came from these choices, or so we thought. We lived in a country where we could sink our teeth into these top-of-the-food-chain choices. By comparison, a glimpse at our Asian neighbors told us their diets were sparse and unappealing. Where were the steaks, the roasted chickens, the cheese and the milk?

In truth, there was miraculous healing power packed into every mouthful of their meals of miso, tofu, tempeh and other soy products, common and readily available in their land of plenty. Researchers eventually noticed that Asian women have markedly lower incidences of estrogen-related diseases and disorders such as breast cancer, PMS and menopausal complaints. Increasingly, investigations have focused on plant hormones in soybeans, substances called isoflavones, or plant estrogens, that have an uncanny ability to duplicate the positive behavior of a woman's natural estrogen supply.

Like the estrogen produced by the body, isoflavones help keep bones healthy and maintain good cholesterol levels. The imprint of these plant estrogens on the body map is not as strong as those of human estrogen, but they have the ability to bind to your body's own estrogen receptors, which can be especially helpful when natural estrogen levels are low.

A great number of fruits and vegetables contain isoflavones, though none has the amount contained in the powerful soybean. For the PMS sufferer and for women in general, some form of soy should become a daily protein staple. In order to reap the benefits Asian women have garnered for centuries from this wonder food, I recommend eating 120 to 150 milligrams of soy each day. It comes in many forms, and there are a wide variety of soy products on the market.

Try to keep an open mind about this change in your diet, especially if the thought of soy initially doesn't seem appealing. Adding one or two daily servings of soy to your diet will help to alleviate the mood swings, irritability and fatigue that go along with PMS.

Action Step: *Many leading food manufacturers are now transforming soy protein into crunchy energy bars and delicious power shakes in an effort to attract the health-conscious but taste-wary consumer. You may be surprised at how much you enjoy some of the products. For other ideas about how to incorporate soy into your meals, see the recipes at the end of this chapter. Don't just expect to "encounter" more soy, make specific plans to integrate it into your daily routine.*

5. Choose your carbohydrates more carefully. Not all carbohydrates are created equal. There are two types, and they have opposite effects on the body's performance, like the "good twin, evil twin" concept.

The "evil twin" carbohydrates are, ironically, the ones most people prefer. These are the simple carbohydrates—white rice, bagels, croissants, pasta, sweets and anything else made with refined flour and/or white sugar. What makes simple carbohydrates "evil" is their roller coaster effect on blood sugar levels. They give a temporary rush of energy as blood sugar quickly climbs, followed by a sudden feeling of fatigue and irritability when it drops just as quickly. For many PMS sufferers, this up-and-down cycle can worsen an already volatile emotional state.

The "good twin" complex carbohydrates are fruits, vegetables and whole grains. They contain abundant amounts of nutrients, along with the energy supplied by carbohydrates. Complex carbs are digested more slowly, keeping blood sugar levels steady. This, in turn, can have a mood-balancing effect on the brain. Complex carbohydrates are your best choice for satisfying PMS cravings. Unlike cookies or a chocolate bar, a piece of fruit or whole-grain toast won't leave you feeling anxious and in need of another "fix" an hour later.

In addition to being rich in nutrients, complex carbohydrates contain a high level of fiber. According to Susan M. Lark, M.D., in her book *Women's Health Companion,* "Fiber binds to estrogen in the intestinal tract and removes it from the body through the bowel movements, thus helping to regulate estrogen levels.... Whole grains also regulate hormone levels due to their high levels of vitamin B and vitamin E, which have a beneficial effect on both the liver and the ovaries."

Action Step: *To receive the benefits of fruit and vegetable fiber, eat them as close to their natural state as possible. Most people enjoy raw fruit but pass on raw vegetables. If this is true of you, try chopping a variety of vegetables into a salad. Or roll them in a whole-grain wrap with a special spread or sauce, such as hummus or tzaziki (plain yogurt, cucumber, lemon and garlic, blended). There are also plenty of low-fat dip recipes that can make eating raw vegetables a treat. When you cook vegetables, try steaming them. Make sure they keep some of their crunch, because the longer they cook, the more nutrients they lose.*

When you're overwhelmed by a craving, go ahead and satisfy it, but do your best to make a healthy selection, preferably one that contains complex carbohydrates. Replace sugar-sweetened foods with those containing a more natural sweetener, such as honey or maple syrup. Opt for a whole-grain oatmeal cookie rather than a chocolate chip cookie. Choose vanilla frozen yogurt with fresh fruit instead of a hot fudge sundae. If it has to be chocolate, try low- or nonfat chocolate milk or chocolate frozen yogurt. Write down your cravings, your responses and ideas for healthier ways to satisfy them.

6. Get the right kind of fat. Many women attempt to eliminate all fat from their diet. This is not a good plan. Fat is necessary for maintaining good health. The key to adding fat to your diet is eating the right kind of fat. And the right kind means those that fall under the umbrella of essential fatty acids.

Essential fatty acids come from seeds, nuts, fish and green leafy vegetables. There are two families of fats—omega-3 and omega-6 fatty acids—that contribute to maintaining good health in numerous ways, from revitalizing the skin with moisture to helping reduce PMS. Good sources of essential fatty acids are flaxseeds or flaxseed oil, pumpkin seeds, sesame seeds, sunflower seeds, walnuts, soy, romaine lettuce, salmon, mackerel and anchovies. Studies have shown that a diet properly enhanced by essential fatty acids can help ease PMS-related headaches, bloating, breast tenderness, mood swings, anxiety and fatigue.

As for oils, I recommend using only olive oil and flaxseed oil, and canola oil when baking something sweet. Cook nonsweets in small amounts of olive oil. Flaxseed oil should not be used in cooking (it doesn't tolerate heat), but you can sprinkle it on top of food such as baked potatoes, roasted vegetables or pastas. Flaxseed meal is also an excellent source of essential fatty acids. It can be added to oatmeal and cold cereal or used in baking. Natural foods markets often carry flaxseed oil and meal.

Action Step: *Write down a weekly plan for adding more essential fatty acids to your diet. Chart your experiences, particularly any difficulties you have in making this change and creative ways to overcome these obstacles.*

7. Add water, water, water. Never underestimate the power of water. Make it your drink of choice before, during and after your period. Even if you experience bloating, you should still drink a lot of water; it acts as a natural diuretic. Water moisturizes your skin and detoxifies your body by transporting waste efficiently. Try to drink sixty-four ounces a day (that would be eight, 8-ounce glasses). If you are active, you will need even more.

Action Step: *How much water are you drinking each day? Guess. Then actually record how much you drink each day for one week. Find ways to increase your intake, such as carrying bottles of water in the car with you, ordering more water in restaurants and taking regular water breaks at work.*

8. Be wary of alcohol and caffeine. Alcohol and caffeine are in the same category, because both do nothing but worsen PMS symptoms. Try to eliminate them from your diet as much as possible. Alcohol causes your blood sugar to drop and can leave you feeling irritable, fatigued and anxious. Caffeine is highly addictive and can increase tension and anxiety, as well as cause insomnia. If you can't seem to stop drinking coffee altogether, try to wean yourself slowly by mixing regular coffee with decaffeinated.

Action step: *It isn't easy to reduce or remove alcohol and caffeine from your diet. A good start is to make a healthy change for one month, and record your responses. Also write down creative substitutes or ways you can adapt your lifestyle to suit these new changes.*

9. Slow down on sodium. Repeated exposure to some flavors makes our taste buds more refined. Other flavors simply become addictive. So it is with the salt in our diets.

Centuries ago, salt was an important preservative that made it possible to store food for daily sustenance. Now, U.S. food manufacturers have turned salt into tasty profits by tempting the American palate in a way that makes taste buds beg for more. Most of the sodium in the American diet comes from salt added during the manufacturing process. The average American diet, due to the proliferation of prepackaged foods as well as the many "fast food" restaurants, contains as much as thirty times the necessary daily sodium intake of about 220 milligrams.

Excess salt turns your body into a sponge. Some sponges inflate to double or even three times their normal size once water is added. By helping the body hang on to water, as a sponge does, excess sodium can add as much as three to five pounds of body weight during the second half of your menstrual cycle. If you're already struggling with other uncomfortable symptoms during this time, why add temporary weight gain to your list of woes?

As you cut back on the salt in your diet, you'll no doubt notice that small changes can really add up to fewer pounds of retained water. In as little as two to three weeks, excess water weight will be eliminated, headaches will occur less often, and many other uncomfortable symptoms brought on by high-sodium living will most likely vanish.

Action Step: *Fresh is always best. Unprocessed foods are naturally low in salt. Try to buy foods in season. In summer and fall, farmer's markets abound with a plethora of fresh fruits and produce. Make this your first stop, before you go to the supermarket.*

Read all food labels carefully. Take note of exactly how much sodium is in your kitchen cabinets. It may be shocking to realize the large amount of salt you consume, often unknowingly. Fortunately, there are an increasing number of natural foods appearing on the shelves at mainstream grocery chains, and the number of health-food stores is also growing, so finding foods that don't contain a lot of salt is no longer difficult.

Know Your Salts

High-Salt Foods to Avoid*

Any food with a label that says "prepackaged"

Any food with a label that says "processed"

Any food with a label that says "preserved"

Instant hot chocolate

Foods containing monosodium glutamate (MSG)

Bouillon cubes

Ketchup

Mustard

Relish

Olives

Pickles

Soy sauce

Worcestershire sauce

Frozen pizza

Pudding mixes

*Read labels carefully and make your own additions to this list.

Foods for Easy Salt-Free Living

Fresh, whole fruits

Leafy greens

Lean chicken, turkey and beef, preferably organic

Rice (found in health food stores and Asian markets)

Asian noodles or pasta

Water, with a squeeze of fresh lemon or lime

Herbal teas, hot or iced

Optimum Food Choices for PMS Sufferers

Protein	Complex Carbohydrates	Fats
Salmon	Whole-grain, unsweetened cold cereal	Olive oil
Mackerel		Flaxseed oil
Sardines	Whole-grain cooked cereals *(oatmeal, rice, millet, quinoa, barley)*	Nuts *(walnuts, almonds)*
Anchovies		
Tofu		Seeds *(pumpkin, sesame, flax, sunflower)*
Tempeh	Whole-grain bread	
Miso	Whole-grain muffins, crackers	
Soy powder		
Soy nuts	Multigrain pancakes and waffles *(Bob's Red Mill and Arrowhead brands are excellent)*	
Raw soybeans		
Legumes *(peas, split peas, pinto beans, garbanzo beans, black beans)*	Pasta made from whole grains, buckwheat, rice, corn, soy	
	Wild rice, brown rice	
	Vegetables and fruit *(fresh and uncooked are the best ways to eat them)*	

Foods to Avoid

Alcohol	Desserts made with re-	Yogurt *(full fat)*
Artificial sweeteners	fined sugar and flour	Foods made with
Beef	Egg yolks	white flour
Butter	Ice cream (full fat)	Foods with artificial
Caffeinated	Lamb	preservatives,
beverages	Margarine	additives and
Cheese *(full fat)*	Milk (whole)	colorings
Chocolate	Palm oil	Foods that are
Cream	Pork	processed, high
Coconut oil	Salt	in animal fat or
Cottonseed oil	Saturated fats	smoked
	Sugar	Fast foods

10. Take time for tea. For thousands of years the people of India have understood the connection between the body, mind and spirit. With this understanding, they created Ayurveda, an intricate system of alternative medicine that combines science (symbolic of the body), philosophy (the mind) and religion (the spirit) to heal the body and promote wellness. The term *Ayurveda* stems from two Sanskrit words: *ayu* meaning "life" and *veda* meaning "knowledge of."

Ayurveda is a fascinating practice to explore further, but for purposes of assistance in alleviating PMS symptoms, we'll confine the discussion in this book to Ayurvedic teas. These have been found to relieve many symptoms related to PMS. Ayurvedic teas can be found at Indian markets or natural foods stores. According to *The Complete Book of Ayurvedic Home Remedies* by Vasant Lad, B.A.M.S., M.A.Sc., the following teas are recommended for PMS sufferers:

- For low backache, lower abdominal pain, distention, anxiety, fear, insomnia and/or mood swings, drink dashamoola tea. Steep 1/2 teaspoon in a cup of hot water for 10 minutes. Honey can be added for sweetness.

- If you have breast tenderness, urethritis, hives, hot flashes, irritability, and/or an occasional burning sensation when passing urine, try this herbal blend: 2 parts shatavari, 1 part brahmi and 1 part musta. Steep 1/2 teaspoon of the mixture with 1 cup of warm water. Drink twice a day.

- If you experience drowsiness and/or retain water to the point that your breasts become enlarged and sore, combine 2 parts punarnava, 1 part kutki and 2 parts musta. Steep 1/2 teaspoon of the mixture twice in warm water. Drink twice a day.

- For stress reduction and relaxation, try any one of these teas: (1) a combination of equal parts of chamomile, comfrey and angelica; (2) brahmi tea: 1/2 teaspoon brahmi steeped in 1 cup boiling water; or (3) tea made of equal amounts of brahmi, bhringaraj, jatamamsi and shanka pushpi. Steep 1/2 teaspoon of the mixture in 1 cup of hot water for 10 minutes. Drink 2 to 3 times a day.

Action Step: *Research where you can get Ayurvedic teas and record your reactions to regular use for two months.*

Recipes to Beat PMS

The following recipes will give you a taste of how to eat for PMS-free living. Try them one at a time, or make them all during your next symptomatic days and find out how they work for you.

Breakfast

Egg-White Scramble

(2 servings)

2 cups chopped vegetables of your choice (broccoli, tomatoes, carrots, purple cabbage, onions, mushrooms, peppers, etc.)
1 egg
5 egg whites
1/4 cup shredded cheese

Sauté the vegetables in a skillet until only slightly crunchy. Beat the whole egg with egg whites and pour over the vegetables. When the egg mixture is almost cooked, sprinkle cheese on top and fold into the mixture. Serve with whole wheat toast topped with honey.

Oatmeal

(I serving)

3/4 cup oats
1/2 cup nonfat milk or soymilk
1/4 cup plain, nonfat yogurt
1/4 cup applesauce
2 tablespoons flaxseed meal (Bob's Red Mill is a good brand)
1 tablespoon honey, optional

Mix dry oats with the milk and microwave for 2 minutes. Add the yogurt, applesauce, flaxseed meal and honey; serve.

Hawaiian Soy Shake

(2 to 3 servings)

3 heaping tablespoons soy powder

1 tablespoon wheat germ

5 ice cubes

1 cup calcium-fortified orange juice

1/2 cup low-fat vanilla yogurt

1/2 banana

1/2 cup crushed pineapple

Put all the ingredients into a blender and mix on high for 30 to 40 seconds; serve.

Lunch

Quick and Easy Hummus Wrap

(1 serving)

Whole-wheat flour tortilla

1 package (6 ounces) hummus mix (available in natural foods stores and many grocery stores)

Olive oil

2 carrots, peeled and cut into sticks

2 leaves romaine lettuce

a pinch of alfalfa sprouts

Dressing

1/4 cup nonfat plain yogurt

1 garlic clove minced

Juice of 1/4 lemon

1/8 teaspoon cumin

1/8 teaspoon cayenne pepper

Recipe continues

Recipe continued

Prepare the hummus mix according to the directions on the package. (Most mixes call for adding 1 tablespoon of olive oil; do not add more than this.) Spread 2–3 tablespoons of the hummus on the tortilla. Add the carrots, lettuce and alfalfa sprouts. In a separate bowl, mix all the dressing ingredients together. Top the tortilla with the dressing and wrap like a burrito. Enjoy!

Easy Bake Tofu Cubes
(4 servings)

1 package (12 ounces) tofu

Marinade

4 tablespoons freshly squeezed lemon juice
2 tablespoons minced gingerroot (fresh is better; if using powdered ginger, use only 1 teaspoon)
1 teaspoon black pepper
Or
4 tablespoons peanut sauce
1 teaspoon soy sauce
1/2 teaspoon curry powder

Use the firmest tofu, drain the water it's in, cut into crouton-size chunks and toss into the marinade. Preheat oven to 400°F. Put on a lightly greased cookie sheet and bake for 20 minutes, until golden brown. Sprinkle the tofu on top of salads or eat separately as a snack.

Spinach Salad with Tofu
(1 serving)

2 cups fresh spinach
1/2 cup sliced red pepper
1/2 cup sliced carrots
3/4 cup Easy Bake Tofu Cubes (prepared using the soy/curry
   version of the recipe on page 127)

Dressing
1 tablespoon white vinegar
1 tablespoon water
1 tablespoon olive oil
1 teaspoon soy sauce
1 teaspoon Italian seasoning
Juice from 1/4 lemon
1 clove garlic, crushed

Combine the spinach, carrots and red pepper. In a separate bowl, mix together all of the dressing ingredients. Pour the dressing over the salad. Add the cubed tofu and toss well. Serve with a whole wheat roll.

Roasted Vegetable Sandwich
(4 servings)

1 eggplant, peeled
1 large zucchini
2 red peppers
2 yellow onions
1 package of whole mushrooms
8 slices whole-grain bread
4 slices of baked tofu (1 for each sandwich)
Olive oil
4 slices of provolone cheese (1 for each sandwich)

Recipe continued

Recipe continued

Preheat the oven to 450°F. Cut the vegetables in large pieces and roast in the oven for 15 to 20 minutes. Meanwhile, toast the bread. Layer the warm vegetables and tofu on the bread slices. Drizzle olive oil over the top and add the cheese. Wait until the cheese melts and then serve.

Crunchy Tuna Salad with Soy Nuts
(1–2 servings)

1 can (8 ounces) water-packed tuna, drained and rinsed
1 cup shredded carrots
1/4 cup red onion, chopped
1/2 cup of feta or bleu cheese
1/2 cup of soy nuts
1/2 cup of croutons

Dressing
1/4 cup olive oil
1 clove garlic, crushed
2 tablespoons lemon juice
1/4 teaspoon black pepper

Add the salad ingredients in a medium-size bowl. Mix the dressing ingredients separately. Toss the salad with the dressing and serve.

Dinner

Poached Salmon Dinner

(1 serving)

4 ounces salmon
1/2 cup nonfat milk
1 lemon wedge

1 cup cut broccoli, steamed
1 clove garlic, minced
1 tablespoon flaxseed oil

1 small baked potato
2 tablespoons nonfat or light sour cream

Heat the nonfat milk to simmer in a medium-size skillet, then add the salmon. Cover the skillet with aluminum foil. (This seals in the moisture and prevents the fish odor from permeating your home.) Poach the salmon on high heat for 6 to 7 minutes. Check the middle of the fish to see if it's done. Cook longer if needed. Sprinkle with fresh lemon juice.

Put the broccoli in a steamer with the garlic. Steam for 8 minutes. Cook longer if necessary; you want it to have a slight crunch. Top with the flaxseed oil. Serve the salmon and broccoli with a baked potato topped with light or nonfat sour cream.

Ground Turkey Soup
(6 servings)

1 medium onion, chopped
1 clove garlic, minced
1 tablespoon olive oil
1 tablespoon Italian seasoning
1 package of ground turkey (the leaner the better)
1/2 cup barley (precooked)
1 cup fresh spinach leaves
1 can chopped tomatoes
1 can kidney or garbanzo beans
4 cups fat-free chicken broth
1 cup frozen peas

In a large pot, sauté the onion, garlic and Italian seasoning in oil until golden. Add the ground turkey; crumble it and cook it thoroughly. Add can of chopped tomatoes and stir. Meanwhile, microwave the barley for 4–5 minutes, and then the spinach for 4–5 minutes, then add both to the mixture along with the remaining ingredients. Cook on low for 1 hour.

Baked Potato, Broccoli and Beans Dinner
(1 serving)

1 large baked potato
1/2 cup cottage cheese
1/8 teaspoon oregano
1 tablespoon flaxseed oil
1/2 cup baked beans
1 cup cut broccoli, steamed

Top the potato with cottage cheese, oregano and flaxseed oil. Serve with baked beans and steamed broccoli.

Sesame Stir-Fry

(3–4 servings)

1 package (12 ounces) extra firm tofu
2 tablespoons black bean garlic sauce
1/4 cup pineapple juice
4 tablespoons olive oil
2 tablespoons minced garlic
1 tablespoon sesame seeds
1 small yellow squash, cut into bite-size 2-inch strips
1 red bell pepper, cut into bite-size 2-inch strips
2 cups of fresh pea pods, sliced into small pieces

Press and cube tofu (see Easy Bake Tofu Cubes recipe above for directions). In medium-size bowl, whisk together the black bean sauce and the pineapple juice; pour over the tofu and set aside. Heat 2 tablespoons of the olive oil in a wok. Add the garlic and cook, stirring until it is lightly browned. Add the tofu to the wok and cook on low heat for 20 minutes. Add the sesame seeds while cooking, and turn frequently to lightly brown all sides. Remove the tofu mixture and set aside in a covered dish. Add the remaining olive oil and vegetables. Stir-fry for 3 to 4 minutes or until the desired texture is achieved. Remove and toss with the tofu. Serve over brown rice.

6 Step 4: Add the Nutraceuticals You Need

GEORGE J. KALLINS, M.D.

I F YOU EAT A HEALTHY DIET, can you get all the vitamins and minerals you need to fight PMS from food alone?

Probably not.

That's what a growing body of research suggests, and my clinical experience confirms that supplements can help many PMS sufferers bring their bodies back into a balanced state.

That's where nutraceuticals come in. Nutraceuticals is a term for vitamin, mineral and herbal supplements that are used to heal the body naturally. They offer an alternative to pharmaceuticals. When used correctly, nutraceuticals pack a powerful punch: the benefits of optimum nutrition combined with the healing effects of medications.

Although there is still a great deal of study to be done in this area, there is a substantial amount of research on the use of nutraceuticals to alleviate many of the major PMS symptoms. Based on existing research and my own clinical experience, I have found that tailoring an individual program from the following six-part nutraceutical "prescription" can help you beat PMS:

PMS Nutraceutical Prescription

Nutraceutical	Suggested Daily Dosage
1. Calcium	1,000 mg*
2. Vitamin B6/ magnesium	Up to 200 mg vitamin B6**/400 mg magnesium
3. Evening primrose	1,300 mg
4. Kava kava	50–150 mg, seven to ten days before your period†
5. St. John's wort	600–900 mg, divided into two or three doses, with meals††
6. Dong quai	Add root to food or drink‡

* Calcium carbonate, in doses of 500 mg or less.

** Toxicity has been noted in high dosages of B6; do not exceed this dosage and stop immediately if negative side effects occur.

† Start with the smaller dose and work your way up to the maximum over several days.

†† Women who are pregnant or breastfeeding should not use St. John's wort. Do not use alcohol or take antidepressant drugs while using this herb.

‡ Take for up to ten days before your period.

The suggested dosages presented here are typical of the ones I have used successfully with my patients. However, it's important that you find the balance that works best for your body. **Consult with your physician before embarking on any of the treatments recommended in this chapter.**

Before you rush out to the health-food store, read the following information about how and when to use each of the elements of this six-part nutraceutical prescription. Your personal plan should be tailored to match your lifestyle, diet and the nature and severity of your symptoms.

Start with Calcium

Recent research has shown that calcium can dramatically erase many irritating premenstrual symptoms including weight gain, depression, unfocused thinking and headaches.

Scientists noticed some years ago that there was an association between low calcium levels in women's diets and the occurrence of PMS symptoms. A recent clinical study undertaken at St. Luke's-Roosevelt Hospital Center in New York City cited conclusive evidence that calcium supplements could be a simple and effective treatment for premenstrual syndrome. In the study, PMS symptoms were significantly alleviated by taking 1,200 milligrams of elemental calcium per day in the form of calcium carbonate.

Do you need calcium supplements? You may, if you're like many American women. Numerous medical studies in recent years have called attention to the dangerously low calcium levels found in the diets of American women. If you're like most busy women—skipping meals and eating on the run—chances are even greater that your calcium intake is inadequate.

The consequences of inadequate calcium in your diet can be severe. Your body needs calcium each day in order to function properly. If it can't get enough calcium from your diet, your body will draw it from the next best source: your bones. Therefore, it's important to replenish your calcium reserves on a daily basis or you'll risk becoming depleted of this vital nutrient.

Action Step: *Getting into the habit of taking daily calcium supplements doesn't require a big investment of either time or money. If you don't consume adequate milk or yogurt products, take 1,000 milligrams of calcium daily. Calcium is best absorbed in doses of 500 milligrams or less. The body can't absorb any more than that at one time. It's easy to find 500 milligrams of calcium in the form of chewable tablets. I recommend taking one with lunch and one with dinner. Avoid taking calcium supplements with calcium-rich meals. Your body will simply excrete what it can't absorb immediately.*

Adding a few of the following foods to your daily diet will boost your calcium levels and may help to correct some of your PMS symptoms.

Calcium-rich Foods

Calcium-fortified orange juice
Calcium-fortified cereals
Low-fat milk
Low-fat yogurt
Green leafy vegetables
Seafood

Try the Vitamin B6/Magnesium Team

Do your mood swings affect your relationships and family life? An irascible temper of a PMS sufferer can come down hard on innocent bystanders, most often spouses and children. The outburst may be completely out of character and leave you with overwhelming feelings of guilt and sorrow, as well as the fear of not having control of your moods—or your life.

Vitamin B6, also known as pyridoxine, may help you regain control over your moods. It helps to elevate levels of serotonin, or the "feel good" hormone, which plays a large role in determining moods and emotions from day to day. Pyridoxine may also relieve PMS symptoms by helping the body produce prostaglandins, hormone-like chemicals that affect mood and various body functions. Low levels of prostaglandins have been linked to PMS-related anxiety and stress-related physical ailments, such as migraine headaches.

The B-Team

Because vitamin B6 is water soluble, it must be taken into your body on a daily basis, either through foods or in supplement form. Your body doesn't store supplies of vitamin B6 from one day to the next.

A true team player, vitamin B6 works best when the rest of the B family of vitamins is also present in the body. In nature, the B vitamins are always found together in food sources, and the synergy among the various B vitamins is especially vital in the area of mood enhancement and leveling off of emotions.

Foods with B6 Bang

Bananas
Cereal (whole-grain varieties)
Corn
Peas
Potatoes
Soybeans

Magnesium Magic

Magnesium works closely with vitamin B6. Magnesium is vital to almost every process your body has to perform. Here's how magnesium works for you on an ordinary morning:

> Breakfast is over and you're heading to the gym. Your meal of cereal, raisins and milk is converted into fuel for your body with the help of magnesium. This mineral also makes possible the hand-eye coordination you need to drive a car. Upon arrival at the gym, magnesium helps your muscles work during the weight-training session and aerobic class. Afterward, magnesium coordinates what it takes to shower, dress, comb hair and apply make-up.

Clearly, your body needs a steady supply of this valuable mineral. In days gone by, magnesium was plentiful in fruits, vegetables and grains, but it may soon vanish from our daily diet. Overfarmed soils produce foods deficient in magnesium, and factory processing removes what little magnesium is left before the food reaches our tables. Although we won't immediately recognize the diminishing levels of magnesium in our food supply, our bodies may. Symptoms of magnesium deficiency include hair loss, mental instability, possible heart conditions, extreme tiredness and a heightened sense of irritability.

Adequate levels of magnesium can help ease some of the most distressing symptoms of PMS: irritability, fluctuating emotions, tension, anxiety and depression. This may be explained, in part, by the fact that magnesium deficiency causes a shortage of dopamine, a chemical found in the brain that regulates mood. Increasing the amount of magnesium in the body with food sources and supplements may help restore dopamine balance.

Magnesium's healing powers are magnified by vitamin B6, potassium and calcium. Vitamin B6 and magnesium work together to ensure proper functioning of the nervous system. Magnesium works with potassium to maintain high energy levels. Magnesium also assists the body with the absorption of calcium and, as an added benefit, can prevent calcium supplements from causing constipation. When these vitamins and nutrients team up, your body may become much better able to handle the symptoms of PMS.

Rich Sources of Magnesium

Cereals
Figs
Leafy greens (preferably organic)
Raisins
Tofu

Action Step: *It is difficult to get sufficient magnesium from food alone. When our food lacks punch, we have to get additional nutrients elsewhere. This is the premise behind the growing use* *of nutraceutical supplementation in the United States. Make a place for magnesium in your medicine cabinet and take 400 milligrams on a daily basis. You should take roughly twice as much magnesium as B6. Therefore, if you take 400 milligrams of magnesium daily, couple it with a 200-milligram dose of vitamin B6. This is probably more vitamin B6 than you can find in a multivitamin or a B-complex supplement. If you prefer to take as few pills as possible, it may be easier to get the rest of your B vitamins from a multi-B vitamin supplement and add a separate dosage of B6 so that you get the full amount you need.*

The Promise of Evening Primrose

In our fast-paced, harried culture, we are often on the lookout for the new drug or gadget that will furnish an easy remedy for all of our ills. We may not find such a panacea in the modern pharmaceutical market, but if we look to the natural healing remedies used in the past by various cultures throughout the world, we may discover new ways to heal modern maladies.

The tiny seeds of the evening primrose offer great promise for promoting health in our day and age. Evening primrose oil was once used as a curative salve on wounds as well as taken internally for stomach ailments and a variety of other problems. Modern herbal science has found that primrose oil can correct a whole host of maladies that seem to stem from low levels of essential fatty acids (EFAs).

According to the *PDR for Herbal Medicines*, the leading reference on verifiable effects of herbal treatments, evening primrose oil has been used to treat skin problems, high cholesterol levels, hyperactivity in children and premenstrual syndrome. This flower provides essential fatty acids in a natural, pure form, and has been proven in several recent clinical studies to alleviate a variety of PMS symptoms.

your body a chance to get acclimated to this herb. Caution: I don't recommend using this herb for extended periods of time. It can occasionally cause allergic reactions and a slight yellowing of the skin.

Soothing St. John's Wort

Used as a medicinal herb since Greek and Roman times, St. John's wort has recently been rediscovered as a mood enhancer for those suffering from depression and PMS-related symptoms. After falling out of vogue for generations, this hearty yellow bud has reappeared as one of today's hottest herbal remedies.

A perennial herb that grows wild along many roadsides, the plant is named for John the Baptist, whose traditional feast is on June 24, the time of year when St. John's wort is in bloom. In ancient times, the herb was widely used to chase away evil spirits and supposedly was effectual in casting demons out of possessed souls.

The word wort, by the way, doesn't pertain to any outlandish growths resulting from its ingestion but rather is the Old English word for plant. The herb's Latin name is hypericum. The use of St. John's wort fell into disfavor in the late 1800s in the United States when many doctors began to discard herbal remedies from their little black bags and replace them with more "modern" patent medicines.

Herbal medications, however, remained in use throughout Europe, where they continue to outsell prescription drugs. Recent clinical studies of the effectiveness of St. John's wort have again boosted this herb's popularity in the United States, bringing this humble healing agent new respect in medical circles as well as among natural healers.

Washing Worries Away

Researchers believe that St. John's wort works much like antidepressant drugs but with fewer side effects. It makes the "good feeling" brain chemicals serotonin, noradrenaline and dopamine more available, which boosts mood. It is increasingly acknowledged by scientists, physicians and other experts that feelings are, in fact, chemically based. St. John's wort is a natural substance that can alter your chemical make-up in a way that alleviates persistent negative feelings. This can be very helpful for the PMS sufferer.

As with any nutraceutical, instant results should not be expected from St. John's wort. Although some subjects have reported feeling a difference in as little as two weeks, in general, it takes two to three months before the full benefits of this herb treatment are experienced. You won't suddenly adopt a giddy attitude toward life. Instead you'll notice a subtle alleviation of tension as time goes by.

Action Step: *Take a 300-milligram capsule of St. John's wort two to three times daily, preferably with meals. Women who are pregnant or breastfeeding should not use this herb. One should also not use alcohol or take antidepressant drugs while using this herb. Consult your doctor before making the decision to switch from antidepressant medication to St. John's wort. If you decide to stop taking conventional antidepressants to switch to St. John's wort, allow your body a three-month cleaning-out period between stopping the drug and starting the herb. Some researchers caution against overexposure to direct sunlight when using St. John's wort, however, the levels prescribed here should not pose a problem in this area. If your skin is sun sensitive, you may wish to take extra precautions.*

Dong Quai: A Girl's Best Friend

Used for centuries to treat women's health problems, the Chinese herb dong quai has been making its way into the medicine cabinets of women throughout the Western world. It is known for its ability to provide relief from both PMS symptoms and menstrual cramps.

she has had good results with using antidepressants for women with severe PMS symptoms. I was so relieved! Now I take a small dose of an antidepressant for two weeks of the month, and for the first time in my life, my mood is stable and I'm fully functional no matter what week of the month it is.

—Marita, mother of three, Minneapolis, Minnesota

In rare cases, the natural approach in steps one through four fails to relieve the symptoms of PMS effectively. It's one thing if you follow the program described up to this point and have a bad month here and there. It's quite another if despite your best efforts to change your lifestyle, you continue to feel out of control. Perhaps your relationships are deteriorating or your job performance is in danger. These are signs that it's time to seek medical intervention and consider the use of prescription medications.

When You Need More Relief

It's understandable that some people believe antidepressants are being prescribed too readily today. In some cases, that may well be true. However, in my clinical experience, few women are interested in using medications unless they have exhausted all other means to treat a serious problem. These are women who fall into the 5 to 20 percent of PMS sufferers whose symptoms are resistant to the lifestyle changes we've described here. In general, they note that exercise and a balanced diet help reduce their symptoms. Nutraceuticals such as calcium and B6 have also proved helpful for many. However, these changes alone have not been enough to successfully treat some of their more severe symptoms, such as mood swings or difficulty in concentrating.

It is important to point out that certain diseases can sometimes appear to be premenstrual syndrome, when indeed they are something else. This is why it is important to seek the care of your personal physician or health-care provider when you believe you're suffering from premenstrual syndrome.

If you've tried our program and your symptoms are still severe, talk with your doctor. He or she should perform a thorough physical examination. Blood tests should also be performed to test for various health conditions such as thyroid disease, diabetes, hypoglycemia and glucose intolerance.

If any of these tests produce abnormal results, then see a qualified specialist who can treat the problem. It is very common for patients who have not noticed any improvement in their PMS symptoms after going through steps one through four to be found to have thyroid disease. Frequently, after fixing the thyroid problem, PMS symptoms disappear.

If all of these tests have normal results, then you probably have a severe case of PMS that requires medication. Modern medicine offers many different types of medications for the sufferer of premenstrual syndrome. Some patients have described some of these new medications as miracle drugs. Surely after suffering from this disease for so long, it seems like a miracle when women can reclaim their lives from this disease.

I prefer to use prescription medications only after steps one through four of our PMS program have not given my patients sufficient relief. Nevertheless, I believe that these drugs are an important weapon in our arsenal against premenstrual syndrome.

Selective Serotonin Reuptake Inhibitors

Probably the most important prescription medications for the management of premenstrual syndrome are those that belong to the category of drugs called Selective Serotonin Reuptake Inhibitors (SSRIs). These drugs include the well-known antidepres-

Team Up with Your Doctor

The most common dosage schedule for SSRI medication used in the treatment of premenstrual syndrome is once daily. However, research has suggested that intermittent treatment during the luteal phase of the menstrual cycle (the two weeks before your period begins) may be more effective than continuous medication throughout the menstrual cycle. Several recent studies have suggested that intermittent administration of citalopram or sertraline may be even more effective than continuous or even semi-intermittent administration of the drug.

Based on these studies, you and your doctor may want to consider trying the intermittent dosing schedule, or taking the medication only during the luteal phase of your cycle. Ultimately some patients may do better on continuous dosing, while others will do better on intermittent dosing. Important considerations when making these decisions include side effects, sexual dysfunction as well as half-life. Furthermore, the clinician will also need to take into consideration whether you will experience symptoms of serotonin withdrawal when stopping the medication during the first part of your menstrual cycle. You are more likely to experience serotonin withdrawal if you are taking an SSRI with a shorter half-life.

It is important to point out that although these drugs are considered relatively safe, they should not be taken or prescribed without close supervision by a physician who is skilled in prescribing these drugs and who also has an understanding of premenstrual syndrome. You will need to work closely with your doctor to monitor effectiveness and side effects, and determine the correct dosage for you. For this reason, it's important that you feel a level of trust and comfort in communicating with your doctor. Don't settle for less when you have the opportunity to take charge of your health and defeat PMS.

It should also be pointed out that it might take several weeks before you see significant improvements while taking these medications. Your physician may decide to start with a lower dose and increase it gradually, to give your body time to adjust. After three to five weeks, you can begin to evaluate whether a particular medication works well for you.

In some cases, these medications can provide the road home to normalcy. And that can be a miracle.

My PMS-Free Life Plan

Step 1: Develop a habit of using mind-body health and fitness practices, including meditation, diaphragmatic breathing and other disciplines such as yoga and t'ai chi, for stress management and mind-body-spirit healing.
I will begin by

_____

on or by (date) _____

Results after one month:

Results after two months:

Results after three months:

Step 2: Find a form of aerobic exercise I enjoy and do it consistently.

Some of my favorite ways to exercise are:

_____

I will help motivate myself to stick with it

*by:*_____

Results after one month:

Results after two months:

Results after three months:

Step 5: If severe symptoms persist, talk to my physician about exploring the use of antidepressant drugs.

Physician I will work with: _____

References

Every effort has been made to secure permissions for material used in this book.

Introduction:
You Can Take Control

American College of Obstetrics and Gynecology (ACOG). "Premenstrual syndrome." *ACOG Committee Opinion Number 155* April, 1995.

Gehlert S., C. H. Chang, and S. Hartlage. "Symptom patterns of premenstrual dysphoric disorder as defined in the Diagnostic and Statistical Manual of Mental Disorders-IV." *J Women's Health* 1999, 8(1): 75.

Kraemer, G. R. and R. R. Kraemer. "Premenstrual Syndrome. Diagnosis and treatment experiences." *J Women's Health* 1998, 7(7): 893–907.

La Forge, R. "Mind-body fitness: Encouraging prospects for primary and secondary prevention." *J Cardiovasc Nurs* 1997, 11(3): 53–65.

Morse, C. A. et al. "Relationships between premenstrual complaints and perimenopausal experiences." *J Psychosom Obstet Gynecol* 1998, 19(4): 182–191.

Tiemstra, J. D. and K. J. Patel. "Hormonal therapy in the management of premenstrual syndrome." *Am Board Fam Pract* 1998, 11(5): 378–381.

Chapter 2
Straight Talk: Why You Feel
the Way You Do

Goodale, I. L., A. D. Domar, and H. Benson. "Alleviation of premenstrual syndrome symptoms with the relaxation response." *Obstetrics Gynecol* 1990, 75(4): 649–655.

Chapter 4
Find the Fitness/Freedom Connection

American College of Sports Medicine. "The recommended quantity and quality of exercise for developing and maintaining fitness in healthy adults." *Medicine and Science in Sports and Exercise* 1990, 22: 265–274.

Kramer, A., S. Hahn and N. Cohen. "Ageing, Fitness and Neuro-cognitive Function." *Nature* 1999, 400: 418–419.

LaForge, R. "The face of women's health research." *IDEA Health and Fitness Source* 1999, 17(10): 43–51.

Morey, S. S. "ACSM revises guidelines for exercise to maintain fitness." *Am Fam Physician* (United States) 1999, 59(2): 473.

Morgan, W., ed. *Physical Activity and Mental Health.* Washington, D.C.: Taylor and Francis, 1997.

Pate, R. R. et al. "Physical activity and public health: A recommendation from the Centers for Disease Control and Prevention and the American College of Sports Medicine." *JAMA* 1995, 273: 402–407.

Tkachuk, G. and G. Martin. "Exercise Therapy for Patients with Psychiatric Disorders: Research and Clinical Implications." *Professional Psychology: Research and Practice* 1999, University of Manitoba 30(3): 275–282.

Chapter 5
Eat to Beat PMS

Greenberg, P. *The Whole Soy Cookbook.* New York: Three Rivers Press, 1998.

James, W. P. T. et al. "The dominance of salt in manufactured food in the sodium intake of affluent societies." *Lancet* 1987, 1: 426.

Lad, Vasant. *The Complete Book of Ayurvedic Home Remedies.* New York: Random House, 1998, pp. 242–243, 260.

Lark, S. M. *Women's Health Companion*. City: Celestial Arts Publishing, 1995, pp. 11, 12.

Sears, B. and B. Lawren. *The Zone: A Dietary Road Map to Lose Weight Permanently, Reset Your Genetic Code, Prevent Disease, Achieve Maximum Physical Performance*. New York: Harper Collins, 1995.

Somer, E. *Nutrition for Women*. New York: Henry Holt, 1993.

Chapter 6
Add the Nutraceuticals
You Need

Brush, M. G. et al. "Pyridoxine in the treatment of premenstrual syndrome: A retrospective survey in 630 patients." *J Clin Pract* 1988, 42 (11): 446–452.

Facchinetti F., et al. "Oral magnesium successfully relieves premenstrual mood changes." *Obstet Gynecol* 1991, 8(2): 177–181.

Nathan, P. "The experimental and clinical pharmacology of St. John's wort." *Molecular Psychiatry* 1999, 4(4): 333–338.

PDR for Herbal Medicines. Medical Economics Company, 1998.

Peirce, A., and J. A. Gans. *The American Pharmaceutical Association Practical Guide to Natural Medicines*. New York: William Morrow, 1999.

Thys-Jacobs, S. et al. "Calcium carbonate and the premenstrual syndrome: Effects on premenstrual and menstrual symptoms." *Am J Obstet Gynecol* 1998, 179(2): 444–452.

Volz, H. P., and M. Kieser. "Kava-kava extract WS 1490 versus placebo in anxiety disorders—a randomized placebo-controlled 25-week outpatient trial." *Pharmacopsychiatry* 1997, 30(1): 1–5.

Ward, M. W. and T. D. Holimon. "Calcium treatment for premenstrual syndrome." *Ann Pharmacother* 1999, 33(12): 1356–1358.

Wyatt, K. M. et al. "Efficacy of vitamin B-6 in the treatment of premenstrual syndrome: systematic review." *BMJ* 1999, 318(7195): 1375–1381.

Heart rate, 101–103

Heart rate monitors, 102

Hindi squat, 66–67

Hummus wrap *(recipe)*, 126

Hypertension, 34, 95

Hypoglycemia, 34, 95

Icon king breathing exercise, 82–84

Isoflavones, 115

Kava kava, 134, 140–142

Knee pump, 64

Law of 10,000 Steps, 105–106

Legumes, 114

Magnesium, 134, 137–139, 144

Mantra, 53–54

Meat, 114

Medications for PMS, 145–151

Meditation, 6, 37–54

    benefits, 38–40

    and exercise, 42–43

    forms of, 41–54

    sound, 53–54

    traditional or sitting, 51–54

Menopause, 95

Menstrual cycle, 16–19

Metabolism, 33, 97

Mind-body exercise, 6, 25–90

    defined, 29

    effectiveness, 26

    safety, 27

    to treat PMS, 27–29

    in Western medicine, 25–26

Mindfulness, 54

Music for meditation, 50–51

Neurotransmitters, 5, 28, 148

Nutraceuticals, 7, 133–144

Nutrition and PMS, 6–7, 110–122

Oatmeal *(recipe)*, 125

Oils, 118

Omega-3 and omega-6 fatty acids, 118, 140

Osteoporosis, 95, 105

Ovaries, 17–18

Ovulation, 18

Paroxetine (Paxil), 148, 149, 150

Pilates method, 86–90

Prana, 28, 32

Premenstrual dysphoria disorder (PMDD), 5, 21, 148

Premenstrual syndrome (PMS)

    causes, 21–23

    defined, 15–16

    diagnosis, 2

    mind-body influences, 5–6, 19, 22–23

    prevalence, 2, 15

    principles for treatment, 4–7

    symptoms, 15–16, 21 *(table)*

    timing of symptoms, 19–20, 24

Progesterone, 5–6, 18, 22

Progressive muscle relaxation, 48–49

Prostaglandins, 136–140

Protein, 113, 114, 122

Prozac, 148, 149

Pulse while exercising, 101–103

Recipes, 125–132

Relaxation posture, 70–72